THE WARS
WE INHERIT

THE WARS
WE INHERIT

Military Life, Gender Violence,
and Memory

LORI E. AMY

TEMPLE UNIVERSITY PRESS PHILADELPHIA

TEMPLE UNIVERSITY PRESS
Philadelphia, Pennsylvania 19122
www.temple.edu/tempress

Copyright © 2010 by Temple University
All rights reserved
Published 2010

Library of Congress Cataloging-in-Publication Data

Amy, Lori E. (Lori Eileen)
    The wars we inherit : military life, gender violence, and memory / Lori E. Amy.
        p. cm.
    Includes bibliographical references and index.
    ISBN 978-1-59213-960-6 (hardcover : alk. paper) — ISBN 978-1-59213-961-3
(pbk. : alk. paper)
    1. Military socialization. 2. Militarism. 3. Violence. I. Title.
    U21.5.A49 2010
    362.82'9208697—dc22

                                                                    2009048501

⊗ The paper used in this publication meets the requirements of the
American National Standard for Information Sciences—Permanence
of Paper for Printed Library Materials, ANSI Z39.48–1992

Printed in the United States of America

2 4 6 8 9 7 5 3 1

For
my mothers
and
my witnesses

Contents

Acknowledgments

he Wars We Inherit maps fifteen years' worth of intellectual, emotional, and psychological spirit-labor. The debts I have incurred over the course of these years and this work are enormous and far-reaching, and I cannot adequately pay tribute here to all those who have helped me in the many dimensions of the labor that this writing has involved. As a work that uses my family life as a frame for critical interrogation and analysis, this book owes its first debt to family and friends. Foremost among those to whom I am grateful are the loved ones who have stood as witness. My mother and my sisters did not choose the path of re-membering that I have taken in this book, but, because I chose it, they have had to walk it with me. They could have abandoned me, but they did not. This labor has been painful for them and often against their will, and it has cost them dearly, but they have stood by me nonetheless. My brothers, each in his own way, have come through as witness. When the work of living seemed too much for me to continue, my nieces, my nephews, and my students inspired me to keep imagining the world I want them to inherit and to work for that.

Denise Wright, my first and most stalwart witness, has offered friendship that has served as anchor, light, ballast, and continuity. This book began with Helen Schluter, who found me as an adolescent in a campground and told me that I could go to college, that I could write, and that I could make a contribution to this world. Helen gave me hope and the intellectual, spiritual, and material resources to imagine and to work toward a future. Donna Waller helped me craft that future at the very beginning of my doctoral studies—I owe her music, play, and beauty. Virginia Evjion brought a kind spirit and Lacanian analysis to my nightmare years. Joyce Dreyfus, my acupuncturist, kept my body going through years of insomnia and participated in the creative process of rescripting nightmares. I owe Kathrin Brantley for the gift of her vision. Through her, I have come to see our lives as works of art and our scars, cuts, and bruises as the raw material from which we craft ourselves. Carla Riley, Jennifer Razee, Liliana Sikorska, Susan Marie Birkenstock, Melanie Almeder, and Dave Russell provided friendship and mirroring throughout the inception days of this writing. Laura Milner had faith in this project from the beginning, and that faith helped keep the manuscript alive. Many of my insights evolved over years of conversation with Angela Crow. As witness, she has been intellectual lifeline and emotional release valve in the work of mourning—a work to which she has contributed books, music, a steady supply of champagne, and my favorite hammock at her fire pit. I owe many thanks to the Georgia friends who have provided various forms of sustenance in these last years, including Dixie Aubrey, Phyllis Dallas, Mary Marwitz, Jim Pugh, Rebecca and John Murray, Anastatia Sims, Constance Campbell, Bekki Davis, Nancy Wright, and Teresa Winterhalter.

The many teachers who have helped me include Ruth Senterfeitt, Roberta Vandermast, and Bruce Hertz from Valencia Community College; they were my first academic mentors in my baby-stepping days. At the University of Hawaii, Cristina Bacchilega was mentor, friend, inspiration, and safe haven. She opened up feminist theory to me—and the possibility of graduate school. I hold her in my heart always, with endless gratitude. At the University of California at San Diego, Masao Miyoshi and Andrew Wright showed me a kindness and compassion that helped me immeasurably. From different directions, each gave me an understanding of history and memory in literature that has helped shape my thinking. At the University of Florida, Elizabeth Langland, Donald and Lynda Ault, and Carolyn Smith were models, guides, and friends. They showed me the kind of human being I wanted to be, gave me tools to shape a career, and continue to help me craft an academic life that I find meaningful. Kate Conway-Turner was professional mentor and friend at a time when the direction of this book and my career were in question. I owe particular thanks to Jim Phelan and his National Endowment for the Humanities (NEH) seminar "Narrative Theory: Ethics in Fiction and Auto/biography." Jim helped me shape the hundreds of pages of writing that were trying to become a book and has been a consistent source of sage advice and good direction since.

I am indebted to the many people who have come into my life for only brief periods of time but who left me with life-changing insights. Kate Millett saw value in my first stuttering attempts to articulate a book and accepted me into the circle of artists working at her art colony farm in Poughkeepsie, New York. Valerie Smith's summer seminar "History and Memory: Recollecting the United States' Civil Rights Movement" catalyzed my thinking about memory work as political, historical, and cultural. Besides providing intellectual stimulation, Valerie's professional advice and personal encouragement were gifts that have helped me with this book, in my career, and as a human being. Jane Vandenburgh combined encouragement with critical reading at West Virginia University's Writer's Workshop. I am indebted to Carolyn Nordstrom for the three days of unparalleled generosity of spirit that she gave to the Southeastern Women's Studies Association's Feminist Locations Conference. Carolyn's work and life remain inspirations for me.

Georgia Southern University provided funding for travel and research for segments of this book. I am especially indebted to the National Endowment for the Humanities for the fellowship support that allowed me to participate in the NEH Seminar on Narrative Theory and to the participants of that seminar, most particularly Jennifer Ruth. I have been gifted with an editor whose vision and insight guided me through revising a manuscript that was still raw when I first submitted it. I am grateful to Mick Gusinde-Duffy at Temple University Press, not only for the potential he saw in an early draft of *The Wars We Inherit* but also for how he saw me. I am grateful to the readers whose input on early drafts of the book helped me shape it—in particular Cassie Premo Steele, whose detailed revision notes were a labor well above and beyond the call of any reviewer.

I finished the revisions to *The Wars We Inherit* while I was in

Albania doing research on gender violence and globalization. In many ways, my work in Albania is the follow-up to the book's call to re-member a future, and I am fortunate to have many friends in Albania taking up this call with me. Special thanks go to Genc Burazeri and Enver Roshi, who brought me to Albania, and to Linda Meniku, my teacher of shqip and strategic advisor. Mirela Cupi, Eglantina Gjermani, Christine Arab, Neta Lojha, and Violeta Azizaj have provided friendship, insight, and inspiration. I owe thanks to Ervin, Dorina, and Heldi Toci for family, vegetable shopping, countless coffees, and sustenance (intellectual and practical) and to the Tresa family—Eni, Enxhi, Luli, and Anna—for family, food, and fun, including dancing lessons and trips to ancient sites, beaches, and restaurants. Special thanks go to the second home I found at Wine Spirit, where Gezimi Baraku, Argert Duro, Erenik Pula, and Sonja Ilia kept me in good food and wine through endless nights of revisions. I am particularly grateful for Gezimi's stories, which bring light and laughter to dark places.

Kashif Tarar, who walked with me through the long years of nightmares, has been a steady source of loving compassion and a partner in the process of working through the histories we carry. I owe him more than can be said here, but I am especially grateful for his insight and perseverance, for his love for my family and kindness to my mother, and for the gift of his family—including the months I shared with Tahira, Asmara, and Zohaib and the many hours I spent on the phone with Humera. Above and beyond all else, I am grateful to Kashif for the gift of ethical witness in the lifelong work of re-membering the futures we have to create.

1

INTRODUCTION

The What and the Why

I have set myself three equally important, and in some ways conflicting, tasks in this book. My first goal is for *The Wars We Inherit* to illuminate the relationship between the violence that we experience in our homes and the ways that we organize our culture. Why is it that one-third of felony assault charges in America are for crimes committed against family members? And why is it that an analysis of inmates convicted of family violence crimes in 1997 reveals that half the convictions were for sex offenses? And how do we explain the fact that, of these sex-offense convictions, 78 percent were committed against females, half were committed against a child under age eighteen, and one-third were committed against a child under age thirteen? Given these statistics, is it a surprise to find that almost half of all women who are murdered are killed by family members? These numbers confront us with the fact that violence in our homes is a pervasive condition of life in the United States. But these violences do not exist in isolation; the violence that we live in our homes is part of the violence in our larger culture, and one of the most important objectives of this book is to illuminate this continuum of violence.[1]

---

1 For sources for these data, see Bureau of Justice Statistics 2005; Centers for Disease Control and Prevention 2009; National Coalition against Domestic Violence 2007.

As a pervasive condition of life in America, violence shapes us. Although some of the violence that shapes us is easily recognizable, such as war and violent crime, the most pervasive violences that impact every aspect of our lives are frequently invisible to us. Researchers and analysts call this violence that is part of the cultural fabric *structural violence*. Structural violences, such as racism, sexism, poverty, and homophobia, commit psychological and physical violence to people by denying them rights in a society and equal access to society's resources. When children in inner cities are denied the quality of education that children in wealthy suburbs receive, when the poor and uninsured are denied the quality of health care that the wealthy and the insured receive, or when poor communities become dumping grounds for toxic wastes, this is structural violence. We fail to understand the nature of this violence, in part because the structures precede us and thus seem "normal" to us and in part because the problem is so big that we do not know what to do about it. A second objective of this book, then, is to help us—college professors, students, the general public—develop the language and the resources for looking at the ways that violence has shaped and continues to shape all of us.

One of the institutions of public cultural violence with which I am most concerned is the military. My father spent twenty-eight years enlisted in the U.S. Army. His life as a military police officer, his tours of duty in Korea and Vietnam, his identity as a "soldier" shaped him. Military identities are defined by a hypermasculinity in which "man" equals the "strong" sex charged with "protecting" (and hence taking charge of) home, nation, women, and children. Another aim of this book is to examine the relationship between the kinds of violences my father brought home—physical, verbal, emotional, sexual—and the militarized hypermasculinity that my father idealized. This militarized hypermasculinity was not just my father's ideal. It pervades our society and functions as an ego-ideal for ordinary boys. *The Wars We Inherit* links our culture's reverence for the soldier, the hero, and the warrior to the violences so commonplace in our homes—the women murdered by their family members and the physical and sexual violence directed against women and children.

The fact that domestic violence in military families is nearly three times higher than in civilian populations allows us to shine a light on one of the structures of violence that is otherwise invisible to us—our gender system. With the understanding that extreme hypermasculinity increases violence against women and children, we can reflect on the less visible, more mundane structural violences that characterize "normal" gender relations in our homes; from this vantage point, it is not surprising that our homes are so frequently the site of private violences inflicted by those people with whom we are most intimate. To do something about the degree of violence we suffer in our homes, at the hands of people with whom we are closest, we must understand and rescript the structural violences of our gender system.

My understanding of the structures and relationships that script the violences we live comes from my study of feminist psychoanalytic theory, cultural and trauma studies, and narrative theory. Since, in American culture, theory tends to be sequestered in the university, my primary audience is college students and the faculty members who teach classes for which *The Wars We Inherit* is relevant. But I believe that these ideas are important to everybody. Hence, my third goal is for this book to be accessible and useful to any person who is working through violence in his or her own life or who is trying to understand violence in our culture.

To make *The Wars We Inherit* accessible to any motivated reader, I use a literary form to tell the story of violence in my own family. I offer this story as a way of illuminating the relationship between the violence that we live in our homes and the violences that structure our culture. But it is important for the book to contribute to the project of helping us imagine futures beyond the violences scripting us. And *imagining beyond* violence requires *analyzing the structures* that evolve violence and the *processes for working through* histories of violence. I have thus included five theoretical interludes that analyze how violence is experienced and remembered, the relationship between military structures and domestic violence, and possibilities for imagining new forms for our individual and social relationships. The interludes are not meant to be exhaustive explanations of the theories from which I have drawn. Rather, they are touchstones to help readers understand why I see what I see and think what I think. Those who are interested in further reading may refer to the References section at the back of the book, which lists the bibliographical citations that correspond to this chapter and each of the interludes. A list of Web sites can also be found at the back of the book.

Fundamentally, this book offers a critical reinterpretation of my own life as a means of encountering and bearing witness to some of the conditions that structure violence in our families and culture. This method poses several challenges, though. First, although I tell stories about my life and family, the stories I tell set up and imply an *analysis* of violence. Hence, this book mimics the genres of autobiography and memoir but has fundamentally different aims. The point of this work is not the *story* but the analysis made possible through the consideration of the stories I tell. Analysis requires thinking about events from multiple points of view and gaining critical distance on emotion and experience. That is, analysis is self-reflexive—it asks us to call ourselves into question. Consequently, this book does not present a unified "story" of my life. Instead, it uses the story form as a way of critically reflecting on emotional experience. Critical reflection insists on evoking—not repressing—ambiguity, contradiction, and uncertainty.

Although I use the story form in a critical way, it is impossible to achieve absolute critical distance on ourselves. I am acutely aware that my own blind spots will reveal themselves to my readers and that, in years to come, I too will be able to see things that are now still invisible to me. This is inevitable, and this inevitability is part of the point this book makes. *The Wars We Inherit* thus uses story not as a way of establishing the "truth" of the past but as a way of tracing emotion backward and of undoing the ego/identity constructions in which we can be trapped. This undoing is the first step toward transformation: We cannot imagine a culture of equality, compassion, peace, justice, and nurturing as long as we are inhabiting identities shaped by the structural violences of patriarchy, racism, nationalism, and global militarism. And we cannot work our way out of these identities and imagine a new social order unless we call the very grounds of our identity formation into question.

Finally, the fact that I write about sexual violence in my family places this book in the midst of highly contentious debates about the nature of trauma and memory. Central to these debates is this question: How much of what we remember is actually "true"? Because much of what has been published in this area relies on reductive arguments and is peripheral to my project, I do not specifically address the memory wars in this book. Instead, I concentrate on illuminating the complex relationship between experience, memory, narrative, identity, and subjectivity. Nevertheless, I am mindful of the battles fought over women's narratives of childhood sexual abuse. Thus, to achieve as much accuracy as possible in my representations, I have relied heavily on my extensive collection of journals and letters to and from my sisters and my father in writing the narrative sections that are first-person, present-tense reconstructions of past events.

The How

The first part of the book reconstructs the family history that the remainder of the book analyzes and works through. Chapter 2, "Frank and Sally," tells the story of my father, Frank, beginning an affair with his niece Sally while his brother (Sally's father) was dying. The crisis of their affair ruptured the lives my family had been leading. During the summer of their affair, Frank brought Sally to Florida to live with us; that fall, he and Sally ran off together, leaving my two brothers and four sisters to take care of my sixty-year-old mother.

I was eighteen, finishing my second year at a community college, when Frank and Sally fell in love. The night Frank brought Sally to live with us, I met a nineteen-year-old boy who said to me, "What happens when all of this blows? You can come to New York with me. You could go to school." I left my older brothers and sisters and the work of taking care of my mother because I wanted to finish college. Chapter 3, "The Hole Things Fall Into," tells the story of my running, for six years, away from the life I had been living. The man I left with, and eventually married, was in the navy, and my life with him recreated the army base life that my mother had lived. After six years of navy life, he received a medical discharge, and we returned to Florida—back to the scene of Frank and Sally's affair, back to everything from which I had been running. Within a few months of returning, I began to have panic attacks. Chapter 4, "Forgetting and Re-membering," tells the story of these panic attacks and the out-of-body experience through which an unwitnessed past emerged into the present. Interlude I, "On the Event without a Witness," explains how traumatic pasts can remain unwitnessed. Drawing on psychoanalysis and recent work in the neuroscience of memory, this interlude uses memory and trauma studies to interpret the experience of violence in my family.

The years I spent running away from my life with Frank only served to re-create, without my realizing it, the structures of violence from which I had fled. The panic attacks forced me into therapy, where I learned to see the patterns I was re-creating. Chapter 5, "Re-membering II," introduces Kathrin, my therapist, and tells the story of returning to my mother and sisters to take up the work of understanding how violence had shaped my family's life and our identities. The process by which my family and I reencountered our pasts is called, in psychoanalytic terms, the work of establishing a community of witness. Interlude II, "On Bearing Witness," traces this process and the theories that explain it. Eric Kandel, winner of the 2000 Nobel Prize in Physiology or Medicine for his research on memory storage in neurons, explains that "most of our mental life is unconscious; it becomes conscious only as words and images" (Kandel 2007, 424). This work of understanding my family's legacy was the work of finding the words and images to bring into consciousness what had remained unconscious in us.

Nightmares have been one of the most painful and difficult routes by which the unconscious exploded into my consciousness. Insomnia, bulimia, anxiety attacks, depression—these were all manageable in comparison. Chapter 6, "If I Should Die before I Wake," explains how my evolving community of witnesses—therapist, friends, family— helped me learn to treat my nightmares as narratives with plots that could, in my dreaming, be rescripted. As messages about the conflicts splitting me, my nightmares have been part of the life-long work of liberating new possibilities for a future that I am still imagining. My past is there, rupturing its way into the present, but the rupture offers a possibility for moving differently into a future that I am in the process of making. I owe a special debt to those who came with me through my nightmare days. Interlude III, "On Bearing Witness to the Process of Witnessing," explains the difficult labor of accompanying somebody in this work. The witness who enters this process walks to the lip of an abyss, to the threshold between past and present. S/he has to remain, steady, holding open the door for the *journey to* and the *return from* the past that must be brought into language. This process of witnessing is the process by which we come to know our buried truths in order to imagine futures with meaning and hope—and it is far from easy for anyone who takes the journey (Laub 1992, 78).

This journey, while not easy, has been my route to repossessing the past that had been possessing me. Chapter 7, "The Pasts We Repeat I: Margaret," and Chapter 8, "The Pasts We Repeat II: Jenny," trace a particularly destructive repetition of trauma that has possessed my family: the trauma of abandonment. My father, who was born in the middle group of thirteen children to a poor family in Massachusetts, was sent to live with an older sister when he was a child. The bad-mother-who-can't-take-care-of-her-children script repeated with my two oldest sisters. Frank sent their children to live with their fathers; my sisters have lived lives bereaved by the loss of their children, and my nieces and nephews have lived lives without their mothers. Interlude IV, "The Uncanny Return," explains this transgenerational transmission of trauma.

If it were easy to see what is unconscious in us, we would not live so much of our lives repeating self-destructive patterns. Chapter 9, "If Our First Language Is the Silence of Complicity, How Do We Learn to Speak?" looks at how we become conscious of the patterns we are repeating and begin the work of imagining new possibilities for living. Weaving together excerpts from journal entries and letters that my father and I wrote to each other, Chapter 9 explores moments of rupture that created the possibility for confronting the fears that kept me and my family silent and complicit. In particular, this chapter emphasizes the crucial role that education played in this process. As a student, I had compassionate teachers who reflected me back to myself in ways that allowed me to see and begin to confront my internal contradictions. As a teacher, I had students who compelled me to find the language to make sense of my experience and the voice to speak up against the cultural conditions that script family violence.

Chapter 10, "The Work of War," looks at my father's violence as the mark of what wounded him and at my family's drama as a microcosm of the culture in which we live. In this chapter, I connect our private family life to some of the most troubling aspects of military life, from military training and service to torture. Interviews with men in the U.S. Navy stationed in Pearl Harbor, Hawaii, address such issues as the sexual practices of naval personnel on leave in the Philippines and Japan, initiation rites for crossing the equator and making a "West Pac" (a six-month deployment in the Pacific Ocean), and the hazing ritual of "oiling" (a practice of anal rape used on nuclear submarines on personnel who have alienated members of a ship's crew). "The Work of War" connects the banal, everyday dehumanizations in our culture—from practices of domination and subordination in our gender and class hierarchies to xenophobia and nationalism—to the militarization of daily life in a war economy.

Extending this analysis, Interlude V, "On the Violence of Nations in the Violence of Homes," analyzes the social contract as a sexual contract that "places the reproductive capacities of women within male-dominated family" structures; the potential for violence—from the family violences that this book traces to the collective violence of war and torture—is written into this construction (Das 2007, 25–26, 45). It is from this critical perspective that *The Wars We Inherit* wants to illuminate the relationship between our individual, interpersonal violences and our public, collective violences: Violence in our homes is a logical continuation of the social order that shapes notions of "home," "family," and "nation."

This violence, however pervasive, is not inevitable. This book maps my personal journey of psychic, emotional, and intellectual growth in order to open dialogue about and suggest directions for social transformation. If we can begin, in our own lives, to transform the destructive ways that we have been shaped by violence, then we might begin to transform the cultural conditions that breed violence. Chapter 11, "Toward Re-membering a Future," explores this relationship between the individual and society—between personal identity, experience, and memory and public institutions, ideologies, and narratives. Following cultural memory theorists, Chapter 11 calls for practices of remembering that cultivate what Tzvetan Todorov calls "exemplary" memory. For Todorov, exemplary memory allows us to transform personal feelings, which are unique and untransferable, into collective and public meanings. Unlike literal memory, which reentrenches pain, anger, and hatred through a static rehearsal of the wrongs we have suffered, exemplary memory connects us to the suffering of others and to the world around us (Todorov 1997, 20). When we can see that all events have a history, a context, a trajectory into the future, we can see that what we suffer is not unique—it is part of a pattern in a social fabric that needs to be remade. Exemplary memory looks for and works at the knots of the social fabric as it loosens the knots of our own pain. It is thus a way of engaging in social action.

Chapter 11 calls for a memory project that brings the past into the present to affirm life over death, love over hate, hope over despair, and compassion over violence. This memory project is founded on the work of mourning. Through mourning, we acknowledge pain and grief and the presence of violence; *by acknowledging* it, we create "a home for the mutilated and violated self of the other" (Das 2007, 47–48). To make *through our mourning* a home for the other bears witness not just to violence but also to the forces of love and life in our relationships: the kind word; the look of understanding; the one who bears our tears without flinching; the one who feels our pain and returns it with a gesture of compassion. Mourning can thus lead us through our pain and to compassion, love, hope. It reestablishes our connections to others and the world. Chapter 12, "The Work of Love," shows how my mother, sisters, and I engaged in the mourning through which it is possible to re-member a future. Here, I return to my sisters and the experience of asking them to talk with me about our lives on army bases with a man who brought Korea and Vietnam home with him. Together, we had to learn how to follow our fear, pain, rage, and shame back to the grieving that we had been deferring.

In Chapter 13, "Conclusion," I bring the work of re-membering Frank and re-membering a future back to the pressing problems of war and violence in our homes. Since I began teaching in 1988, I have worked with at least five students a semester who bring to my classes and to their work histories of rape, murder, incest, war, battery, self-inflicted injury, and multiple other forms of individual and cultural violence. In the past few years, I have been particularly affected by my students returning from Iraq—returning to a vacuum of silence that cannot bear witness to or help them encounter the truth of their experiences. In the upcoming years, we shall have to confront the consequences to ourselves and to the rest of the world of the U.S. "war on terror"—a war that has unleashed massive violence that will affect us for decades to come. If we do not want to watch the continued destruction of our lives and worlds, we have to find ways to understand and work through the violences that we inflict.

I do not know whether, as a species, we will be able to do this. But I *do* know that we have as much capacity for connection, compassion, and loving relation as we do for killing, hatred, and violence. Our machinery of death and destruction did not come easily or "naturally" to us—we have had to work long and hard for it. We have spent centuries inventing, training, practicing, preparing, and sacrificing to make war. In contrast, we have devoted little of our energy and few of our resources to cultivating the practices and tools for living in peace. We have to work as hard to forge nonviolent ways of inhabiting this world as we have worked to make war. To make peace, we have to train our hearts and minds, and we have to practice self-reflection, analysis, and compromise in our day-to-day lives. *The Wars We Inherit* is my contribution to this project.

2

FRANK AND SALLY

I still haven't figured out what to say to people when they ask me about my father. I've tried "he's disappeared"; "he's a casualty of war"; "he's a bastard and I haven't seen him since 1983"; "he's a wounded soul, lost in this world." Anything I say violates social etiquette. But he is my childhood, my adolescence, a presence shadowing me. If I hide him or lie about him, I hide parts of myself and lie about who I am. To find the words to speak about my father is to allow us both our integrity.

My search for a way to explain Frank always brings me back to the summer of 1982, when I was eighteen—the summer of Frank and Sally.

When Frank disappeared in September of 1982, it was with his niece Sally. He and Sally met again that spring, in Lowell, Massachusetts, when Nathan was dying. Nathan was Sally's father and Frank's older brother. When Nathan was dying and Frank and Sally were falling in love, I was back in Florida with my mother, finishing my second year at a community college in Orlando. I was eighteen, the only one of my mother's seven children still "at home"—living in a trailer in Southport Park, the campground Frank ran in Kissimmee. I have no way of really knowing what happened in Massachusetts or what made Frank and Sally fall in love. All I have is the story Frank and Sally told me. The way I heard the story, Nathan was close to dying by the time Frank was called. But Nathan didn't go quickly or easily. He lingered, borderline, with cancer eating away at his body and pain clouding his mind. I don't know whether this information is true. When it wasn't exaggerated, a lot of what Frank said was just plain made up. But, true or false, the way Frank and Sally told me the story, they wanted to end Nathan's suffering and let him die with dignity. In their story, the rest of the family wanted to artificially prolong Nathan's life, putting him on life support and dragging his suffering out. In their own eyes, Frank and Sally were the "good" guys, righteous. By the time Nathan died, Frank and Sally had united in a fight against the rest of the family, who had become the enemy.

What does it mean for a fifty-five-year-old man and his forty-five-year-old niece to fall in love while they fight to keep a brother-father off life support? What did this dying mean to them? What did it open up?

Frank had been out of the army for just over ten years when he went back to Massachusetts to watch Nathan die. For ten years, he had been moving from fish camp to campground up and down south and central Florida, living out his desire to get "away from civilization" and "back to the land." We lived a few years in a campground on Bahia Honda, a tiny island in the Florida Keys, and a few years in a fishing camp on Lake Okeechobee, at the edge of the Everglades. When Frank remet Sally, we were living in a campground that was six miles down a dirt road. To get the mail or to go to school, we had to drive fifteen minutes to the paved road, as neither the mail truck nor the school bus would drive across that much dirt to get to us.

Something happened when Frank went back to Massachusetts—something about Nathan dying and remeeting Sally, something about returning to his childhood home and the family he had left behind. Something made Frank and Sally fall in love, made their skin crawl under their clothes, made them peel their old lives off.

In retrospect, I think that Frank had been boiling over since he got out of the army. I think we kept moving from campground to campground, chasing Frank's desire to get "back to the land," because he could not make sense of how to live in the world without the army to provide structure for him. After almost thirty years in the army, after Korea and Vietnam and defining himself as a "soldier," after living and breathing the Cold War, I think Frank needed an enemy to fight. I think he needed his anger, a righteous rising up against injustice that he used to hold himself up, to give him meaning in the world.

In the army, Frank was an MP (military police). I think he liked that—liked that he could find people who were breaking the law and punish them. This is purely conjecture on my part. Frank retired from the army when I was in the second grade, and I remember very little of our life on military bases. I speculate that he liked his identity as an MP based on the way he policed the campgrounds in which we lived. He rode around in the park truck looking for signs of disobedient campers. Once, believing that cars were driving on a road marked "no trespass," Frank spent hours in his workshop studding two-by-fours with long, piercing nails. I remember him going out to line the road with these boards, full of "this will teach them a lesson" and "I'll show them." He took pleasure in the thought of ruptured tires and of these trespassers being punished.

In retrospect, I think Nathan's death gave him a real fight again, with a moral to it: death with dignity. He and Sally were the troops, the good guys in a showdown against the enemy, which this time was the rest of the family.

But this is retrospect. When Frank was in Massachusetts, I didn't see any of this. What I did see confused me. I couldn't make sense of it.

A SCENE

Frank sequesters me in the back of the trailer, between the clothes-line and the utility shed. He shows me a pair of ruby earrings, heart shaped, that he's gotten Sally for Mother's Day. He has just come back from Massachusetts. Nathan is dead, and I've only recently learned about his daughter, my cousin Sally. Once, when Frank called from Massachusetts, he put me on the phone with her. He said, "Here, talk to your sister." We were twins, Frank said. Ruby is my birthstone, and these earrings he is showing me are for my cousin, for Mother's Day.

Sheepishly—or maybe surreptitiously?—he pulls out an identical set, for Mother. "I don't want your mother to get jealous," he says.

"They're pretty," I say.

A PROLONGED SCENE

Frank is on the phone with Sally. We've never had a private line in the trailer before. Since Frank began managing state parks, we've always had an extension of the park office phone. I like these phones. They're old fashioned, with a big bulky base that has a row of light-up buttons on the bottom: one for hold, two buttons for the two different lines ringing into the park number. We could use the phone for personal calls when the park was closed as long as we were careful to answer business calls as well. From the office, Frank could pick up the phone and listen in on our conversations. When Frank got back from Massachusetts, he installed our first private phone line. I think this new phone is sleek, modern. It has a brown plastic base that lies flat on the end table, with a long cord that lets you walk around the house with the oblong receiver. Frank spends several hours a day walking around with this phone, talking to Sally.

Sometimes, he gives the phone to me so I can "get to know" my cousin. I never know what to say. Sally says, "Your father is my savior. I just don't know what I would have done without him. Nobody else understands." Sometimes, she says, "We are grieving."

I didn't know Nathan. I'd met him, once, when my father took us back to Massachusetts for his mother's funeral. I was twelve. I wasn't grieving. I didn't remember that he had a daughter. I wasn't sure what I was supposed to do with this newfound cousin.

Mother is jealous. Periodically, she asks me, "What do you think they talk about?"

"They're grieving," I say.

In May 1982, less than a month after he got back from Massachusetts, Frank took Mother and me to California to visit Sally and her family. From my point of view, they were rich. Sally's husband, Douglas, was a vice president with a large computer firm, and they lived in a wealthy neighborhood ten minutes outside San Jose. Douglas and Sally had five kids: Stephanie, the oldest, was married and had a family; Doug, the first son, was away at college; and Mark, Kendall, and Melissa were teenagers living at home. I don't know what Sally's family thought about this newfound uncle and the wife and daughter who were supposed to spend the month of May with them. I was awkward, feeling the distance between the campground we lived in and their million-dollar home in Saratoga. The master bedroom, where Mother and Frank were supposed to sleep, had a sunken tub with gold faucets. A separate shower was on the right-hand wall, and there was a long counter with double sinks made of marble. Their bedroom was as big as our whole trailer, with a walk-in closet lined with mirrors that made the room seem even bigger. Sliding glass doors opened onto the patio and pool. I'd never seen anything like this before.

All these years later, the rest of the house is a blur to me. But I retain an image of this bedroom, scene of my mother's humiliation.

CALIFORNIA SCENE I

It is our third day at Douglas and Sally's, and I'm still awkward and insecure. Douglas is nice to Mother and me, but he seems to dislike Frank. He interrupts Frank a lot, and they seem to have a one-up you thing going on. Frank swaggers. They all drink. Mother keeps asking me questions about Frank and Sally: "What do you think they're talking about?" and "Where are Frank and Sally now?"

In a few days, Douglas has to go out of town on a business trip. We're supposed to go to dinner tonight. Mother loves going out to restaurants, and she is happy about this. Mark is working, and I don't know where Kendall and Melissa are. It's just Frank and Sally, me, Mom, and Douglas who are going. I have a bad feeling.

At the dinner, Sally is drunk. She's going on and on about how hard her father's death was, how her Uncle Frank is the only one who was there and who helped her, he saved her, she just doesn't know what she would do without him. Douglas is irritable and short. Finally, he interrupts Sally. He says, "You also had us. The kids and I were here to support you."

Sally raises her voices and shrills, "You weren't there! You don't understand!"

Douglas is angry. Frank rises up, as though to protect Sally. Mother is conciliatory and says that they don't mean anything and we should leave now.

I'm embarrassed. Frank and Sally are drunk, Douglas and Frank are fighting, and Mother is pleading. Everybody is loud. People are looking at us. The waiter brings the check, and Frank fights with Douglas about who is going to pay it. Frank wants to show he is as good as Douglas—he has money, he can pay. Douglas says, no, we are his guests, he will pay for dinner. Frank is fighting to be the big guy, the hero. Douglas is fighting to put Frank in his place. I want to find a back door, sneak out, be alone, get away from here, and get back to Florida.

Finally, we are outside the restaurant. Frank and Sally won't get in the car, though. They tell Mother, Douglas, and me to go home. They say they will walk, that it's a nice night, and that it's not that far. Douglas protests and tells Sally to get in the car. It's getting harder for him to control his anger. Mother can't issue an order like Douglas. She tries reason and pleading. Nothing works. I climb into the back seat and wait.

Frank and Sally start walking.

Douglas says, "Come on, Dee, let's go," and he gets in the car.

Back at Douglas's house, Douglas asks Mother if she's noticed anything odd about the way Frank and Sally are acting.

"I know Nathan's death was hard on them," Mother says. "They are grieving."

"It's not normal, Dee. Something is wrong."

Douglas has noticed that Frank doesn't sleep in the master bedroom with Mother. He and Sally stay up all night, drinking and talking, with the lights off. When Douglas asks Sally to come to bed, she says she can't, she's too upset.

"It's a phase," Mother says. "It will pass."

Douglas goes into his study. Mother goes to bed. I find a book, sit down at the dining room table, and begin to read. Nothing makes sense to me. I reread the first page over and over, but the words don't stick. Finally, I turn the page anyway. When Frank and Sally come home, I'm still at the table, reading words that do not keep their meaning.

They're still drunk. More drunk. Can they be more drunk? Where have they been? I don't want them to breathe on me. I don't want them to touch me.

They sit down, Frank beside me and Sally across from me. Sally takes my hands.

"Your father and I have something to tell you," she says.

This is what they tell me.

"We are in love," Frank says. He knows I will understand. He knows that I know how much he has suffered, how he has sacrificed his life for Mother and for us kids, and how he has never had anything for himself.

He says:

"I've given everything I have to all of you, and I've never asked for anything for myself."

"Your mother doesn't understand me. She never has. It's impossible to talk to her."

"I give and give and give, and it is never enough. No matter what I do, it's never good enough,"

"Finally, I've found somebody who understands me."

Sally says:

"Your father helped me get through my father's death. Nobody can know what I suffered. Your father was my only comfort, the only one who understood."

"After Daddy died, the rest of the family treated us like it was our fault. At Daddy's funeral, your father and I had to hold onto each other—we're the only family we have left now."

They say:

"We know you will understand. You are the only one we can tell, the only one who will understand what we are going through. We know we can count on you."

Sally is still holding my hands. I let them lie there. They look at me like they are expecting something from me. I'm not sure what I'm supposed to understand, what they're counting on me for. Like the book I have just been reading, their words drift away from me and lose their meaning.

Frank asks, "Do you understand?"

I nod.

This is what I understand: I am a particle of water in the ocean. I am a dolphin swimming at sea, and they are flailing limbs bobbing on the surface above me, their words fading in and out in relation to the noise of their splashing. They are colored specks that I see from my underwater place, distorted by the sheets of water separating them from me.

———————

That summer, I was eighteen, with two years of a general education from Valencia Community College, dreams of going to a university, and eighteen years of being Frank's "baby," the "apple of his eye," and the only one who "understood" him. I was a "good" girl—I always did what Daddy told me. I never rebelled. My sister Georgia rebelled. And she got hit—and eventually thrown out of the house.

Frank was always mad at Georgia for something. Her skirt was too short, she was too sarcastic, she stayed out too late, she talked back, she left a speck of egg on the breakfast plate, she didn't get the glasses clean, she didn't take anything out of the freezer for dinner, she didn't hang the laundry out to dry, she didn't mop the floor, there was dirt under the rocking chair, there were dirty dishes in the sink, she lied to him, she snuck out with boys.

The day Frank threw my sister away, he was mad at her about Caesar, her German shepherd. He found dog shit in the campground and said that it was Georgia's fault, that she could not be trusted to clean up after her dog. Georgia explained that she had cleaned up after Caesar, that there were a lot of other dogs in the campground, and that this wasn't her fault. Everything she said just made Frank angrier. He handed her a rifle and told her to shoot Caesar. Georgia teared up, but she wouldn't plead with Frank. She'd had so many years of his screaming and yelling, so many bruises from his hitting, that she didn't want to let Frank see her cry any more. She didn't want him to have that kind of power over her. She choked her tears back and stood up to him. No, she said—no. She wasn't going to shoot her dog.

This was the last standoff between Frank and Georgia. He was in a rage, cussing at her and calling her names. Finally, he told her to get out of his sight—she was dead to him, and he never wanted to see her again. Georgia took him at his word and left. After she was gone, Frank dressed in black, said his daughter was dead, and forbade any mention of her name in his house. Mother and I acquiesced.

When I was twelve, I could see Georgia, six years older than me, asleep under Buckhead Bridge. In between having a bed in our trailer and finding a friend to stay with, this is where she lived. I cannot speak for Mother and cannot presume to guess her reasons for remaining silent while her daughter lived under a bridge a half mile from our trailer. As for me, I knew I didn't want to live under a bridge. I didn't know how I would eat, take a bath, go to school, or take care of myself. I didn't want Georgia to live under a bridge, either. But I was twelve and afraid—I was no help to her. I didn't have the courage to stand up to Frank. I was complicit.

Where does complicity begin?

At five years old, when you promise not to tell?

In a basement in Alaska, afraid of the huge metal jaws of animal traps used to trap elk and mouse and caribou, traps that are bigger than you?

At eight years old, watching your father break down and clean his guns, lovingly polishing his precious black metal?

At ten years old, listening to your father tell you that he'd give anything to be back at war, in a "firefight," killing "gooks," but the army doesn't want him anymore and there are no more wars to fight?

When you are old enough to understand that it is your job to make your father feel like a "man"?

Once we have learned the silence of complicity, how do we learn to speak?

In 1982, I was still complicit. I was Frank's accomplice. From my underwater place, I was still twelve, wishing Georgia back in our room and out from under Buckhead Bridge. I didn't say "incest." I didn't say "no." I didn't tell. I kept Frank and Sally's secret. It never occurred to me to seek Douglas's help, to tell Mother, or to confront Frank and Sally with the meaning of their actions.

A few days after the fight at the Chinese restaurant, Douglas went to Japan on business. Mark was busy with his job and classes at the local community college. Kendall and Melissa were in school all day and out with their friends in the evening. For two weeks, without other witnesses, I was Frank and Sally's accomplice. I was their excuse to sneak away.

CALIFORNIA SCENE II

Frank and Sally tell Mother that I want to go to the beach, and they are going to take me. Mother wants to come too. No, they say. She should stay home. To get to the beach, we have to climb up dunes, and Mother can't make that climb with her arthritis. I feel guilty, like I'm betraying Mother. I want to stay home and be left alone. But I don't say anything. I get in the car and drive with Frank and Sally to a beach in San Francisco. As soon as Frank and Sally have laid out the blanket and unpacked the picnic basket, I leave to walk along the beach. When I come back, I see Frank kissing Sally's arm. He starts at the tips of her fingers and kisses his way up to her throat, kissing a line along her arm in the same way you eat a row of corn off the cob.

Years later, when I tell my friend Helen about this day, she says she used to see Frank do that to me. She always thought it was strange.

Before we go back to Sally's house, we drive across the bridge to Sausalito. I calculate the distance from the Sausalito bridge to the water below. I wonder if I have the courage to get out of the car and jump. Georgia would have that courage. I don't. I'm a coward. I remain silent, complicit.

When we get back to Douglas and Sally's house, Mother is drunk. She asks me, "What is going on?"

"Nothing," I lie.

A few days later, Douglas comes home. Douglas's brother, Ron, is bringing his family to California for vacation. I'm relieved. Ron, his wife, and their two teenagers will be with us during the day, so I won't be alone with Mother, Frank, and Sally anymore. The day they arrive, I go to the airport with Douglas, Kendall, and Melissa to pick them up. I know I shouldn't—I know I shouldn't leave Mother home alone with Frank and Sally. But I go anyway. When we get back, Frank and Sally are at the bar. I don't see Mother.

I ask, "Where's Mom?"

"She doesn't feel well," Frank says. "She's lying down."

Sally says Mother's stomach hurts. She thinks something she ate didn't agree with her.

I go into Douglas and Sally's bedroom, where my mother sleeps. At first, I don't see her. I hear what sounds like vomiting. Then I see her, reflected in the full-length mirrors on the doors of the walk-in closet. She is in the bathroom, on her hands and knees, throwing up in the toilet.

"Lori? Is that you?" Her voice is breaking.

I lock the bedroom door and walk into the bathroom. Mother sags across the toilet bowl, arms clutching the porcelain rim, nose pressed into an elbow, trying not to breathe in the toilet smell. Her glasses are sliding off her face. She is fifty-nine and heavy, and the loose flesh on her arms flattens out as it presses against the toilet. She is in her bra and a pair of black stretch pants. She sobs, and her flesh shakes. She is humiliated and in pain.

I clean Mother's face and wipe away the vomit on her neck and shoulders, around the toilet, on the bathroom floor. I take the rest of her clothes off and put her nightclothes on. I bring her to the bed, place a cold washcloth on her eyes, and put a wastebasket by her. I kiss her forehead. "I love you," I say. She says, "My baby." She's worried that I will think badly of her.

Out of the sliding glass doors, I see a broken wine glass. Red stains crawl across the pale cream and blue pool tile. I want to protect my mother and help her. I love her. I want her to protect and help me. I hate her. I hurt for her. I'm hurting her. I'm a coward, complicit. I'm floating underwater again, reaching through the membranes separating me from these things on the surface: Frank, Sally, broken wine glasses, my mother throwing up in her bra and black stretch pants.

I go to the pool and pick up the fragments of glass, wiping away the red stains. I shut the curtains. I go back into the living room. Everybody is there.

Douglas asks, "How's Dee?"

"Fine," I say. "Her arthritis medication upset her stomach."

I swallow my vomit. I smile. I hate myself. I want to die. But I'm a coward. I don't have the courage to kill myself. I don't have the courage to live under a bridge. I'm not Georgia. I'm silent, complicit. I stay home, pick up broken things, and clean up the mess.

A few days later, I borrow Sally's Cadillac to take the teenagers, my newly discovered second cousins, to dinner. When we get back to Douglas and Sally's house, police cars are there. Lights are flashing. Everybody is outside. Douglas is yelling.

"I want to know what is going on!" he demands. "This is my wife and my house! Frank, you are sick! You and Sally need help!"

Sally screams, "You don't understand me! Only Uncle Frank understands! What we are doing is nobody's business but ours!"

Frank is yelling at Douglas. He is going to beat Douglas up, to kick the shit out of him. Ron tries to intervene. Frank says he will beat the shit out of him too. The police don't seem to know what to do. They are embarrassed. This is a rich neighborhood, Douglas is rich, and they are not sure if a crime has been committed here or how to handle it. Mother is begging everybody to stop yelling, to come back inside and be nice. I don't know who called the police. Frank, still yelling and threatening to beat people up, comes over to me and takes Sally's car keys. Frank and Sally get in her car and drive away.

Douglas gets in his white BMW and chases after Sally's yellow Cadillac. The police leave. The rest of us don't know what to do.

———

I spent the rest of the night driving around Saratoga with Kendall, my seventeen-year-old second cousin. Kendall liked his Uncle Frank. He couldn't believe Uncle Frank and his mom were doing anything "like that." I didn't tell Kendall about the beach or about the night Frank and Sally got drunk and walked home from the Chinese restaurant and then told me they were in love. When Kendall consoled me, telling me not to worry and assuring me that we would find his mom and Uncle Frank and clear all this up, I still didn't say anything. I just got in his Bobcat and rode around all night, looking for Sally's yellow Cadillac.

Shortly after daybreak, Kendall finally gave up. When we returned to his house, we found Douglas and Mother at the kitchen table—waiting for us, waiting for Frank and Sally, waiting for their world to return to normal. Mother was distressed but not crying—she was "holding up." (It would take six more years before I could realize, remembering this night, that we were both in shock.) Douglas, Kendall, and I compared notes—the places we'd gone and the times we'd been there.

We couldn't think of any place to look where we hadn't already been or anything to do that we hadn't already done. There was nothing for us to do but keep waiting.

Twenty-four hours later, Frank and Sally still had not returned. No phone call saying, "We're all right" or telling us what to expect. After a night haphazardly driving around Saratoga and a day in limbo and waiting, we had to inch our way out of numbness and denial. Douglas had to go back to work. Mother and I had to get back to Florida. We pooled our resources: I had $90 left from the money I'd saved working as a student assistant at Valencia Community College, and Mother had a Diner's Club credit card in Frank's name. We had our airline tickets for the return flight, dated for the following week. Douglas had to help us make arrangements—for a hotel, for stand-by seats on a flight back home, and for rides to the hotel and airport.

Mother and I returned to Florida the third week of May 1982. We returned with a combination of denial, shock, numbness, crying, with the threads of our identities unraveling.

For the next two weeks, we lived inside the gaping hole of our incomprehension, floundering in our helplessness. Mother hoped Frank would come home and that she would be able to forget everything that had happened in California. She wanted to "make up" and go on with her "normal" life. She'd done it before: in Massachusetts, after the police investigated Frank for molesting her oldest daughter; when she sold her house and followed Frank back into the army, when he went to and came back from Korea, twice; when he went to Vietnam and came back with his Vietnam tan. Always, after times like the Thanksgiving when I was eleven or twelve and Frank threw her and Georgia out of the house, things had "settled down." The anger or the alcohol wore off, the guns didn't kill, the life-threatening eruptions lost their force, alarm clocks rang, and work and school and making dinner called. Life "went on."

I got a job waiting tables at the local IHOP. Mother called the rest of her children, who gave what help they could—money, if they had it, comfort, reassurance. The phrase she kept repeating, her mantra, the thing that carried her through the worst days after Frank and Sally: At least I have my children. Seven of us. She had three daughters from her first marriage: Margaret, Bernie, and Zane. Margaret was in her forties, working as a nurse and living in a campground not far from us. Bernie lived with Margaret. Zane had just returned from Germany and was living on an army base in Georgia. She had her four children from Frank: Mike, Leonard, Georgia, and me. The boys lived in South Florida, a few hours away. Georgia, the sister closest in age to me, was twenty-four, living with her husband and newborn son in a trailer park in Davenport, a half-hour's drive from Mother.

Mother's children helped her, but it was hard on them. In 1982, none of my sisters and brothers had money. We were all struggling through the same histories: itinerant lives on army bases and in campgrounds, Frank's violence, different versions of shock and denial. But each of my brothers and sisters rallied around Mother, giving her whatever they could spare—time, love, labor, any cash they could scrape together.

Mother had her children, except for me. I had neither comfort nor reassurance for my mother. I maintained my silence, remained Frank and Sally's accomplice.

Two weeks after Mother and I returned to Florida, Frank finally came back. He wouldn't say much about the time he had been away. He still denied, to Mother and to the rest of the world, that anything was "going on" between him and Sally. They had their story: Nathan died, the family turned against them, they were the only family they had left. And I never contradicted it. Not even when, less than a week after he returned, Frank flew Sally out to Florida so they could be together.

The night Sally flew in from California, I admitted my mother to the hospital. She was having pain in her chest. Frank wouldn't take her; he said she was faking and just wanted attention. When I got her to the hospital, the Emergency Room doctor admitted her immediately; Mother had had a heart attack ten years before, and they had to monitor her.

I stayed with Mother until the paperwork was done, until the sedatives took effect and she drifted off into the first real sleep she'd had since California. When it was clear that Mother was not in immediate danger, I couldn't make myself go back to our trailer—to Frank and Sally, to that incomprehensible place of crazy making. From a payphone in the hospital lobby, I called Kim, an old friend from high school. I asked her to drive out to Cocoa Beach with me.

"You're crazy. A hurricane is coming in—we can't go to the beach."

"I can't go home."

"You can come to dinner with me and Jason if you want."

Jason, Kim's boyfriend, was in nuclear power training school at the Naval Training Center in Orlando. I drove the forty-five minutes from Kissimmee to Orlando to have dinner with Kim and Jason at Perkins restaurant. That was the night I met Lewis. He was in school with Jason and looking for an excuse to get off the base. He came to dinner with us, where I told them all about Frank and Sally—everything, all the things I couldn't tell my family.

After dinner, Lewis went with me to Cocoa Beach. I didn't care whether the wind blew my car off the road, didn't care whether I was eaten by sharks, and didn't care whether the current dragged me into the ocean and took my life away from me. Part of me wanted to lose myself in the rain and the wind and the ocean, lose myself in a way that would let me stay asleep forever, let me never have to wake up and find my mother in the hospital and Sally in my mother's room with my father. But the car didn't wreck, the ocean didn't swallow me, and the tropical storm didn't quite make hurricane force. The rain soaked me, and I was too chicken to swim and tempt the sharks. For a few hours, though, the wind soothed me and brought the forgetting I was seeking.

The predawn hours took my forgetting away. I had to drive Lewis back to the base and return him to the navy, then drive back in the direction of Frank and Sally. The things I was trying to forget were still there, waiting for me to go back and face them. (Except, I couldn't do it, couldn't "face" things—not then. Not for six more years.)

For the week that my mother was in the hospital, I spent days with her, evenings with Lewis, and nights at my friends' houses or in my car. When Mother got out of the hospital, Sally moved out of my mother's bedroom and into my father's van, which he parked in a campsite within sight of our trailer. Lewis had come with me, once, to visit Mother in the hospital. He came to our trailer the weekend Mother came home. He met Frank and Sally.

"That's fucked up," he said. "What's going to happen when this whole thing blows?"

"I don't know."

"You can come to New York with me if you want. You could go to school."

I was eighteen, and he was nineteen. Two months later, I took my college transcripts and my peek-a-poo dog, packed my books in a small U-Haul, and drove away. I left my mother my Toyota Corolla: my guilt offering before I bailed.

On the way to New York, in the bathroom of a Burger King, I stood next to a high school girl throwing up in the sink.

She asked, "Do you drink?"

"Sometimes," I said.

She paused to vomit and then continued: "Don't ever drink," she said. "It's not worth it."

In the bathroom of a Burger King, next to a fifteen-year-old girl puking her guts out, on my way to New York with a man I just met, I thought, "I'm fucked. I'm just fucked. Fucked fucked fucked fucked fucked fucked fucked. Just fucking fucked."

The girl left. I swirled her vomit down the drain, washed my face, and went back to the car. It was late and dark. It was my turn to drive. I drove us up I-95, toward the New Jersey Turnpike, on the way to Ballston Spa, New York.

A month after I left for New York with Lewis, Frank ran off with Sally. The day he left, a park ranger in the fish camp we lived in brought Mother a note that Frank had left on his desk. It was his resignation. Frank never told Mother he was leaving. He didn't say goodbye. He didn't leave her any money, make arrangements to move the trailer out of the campground, or help set her up in a new life. Mother found out her husband had left her, with no help or hope or way to think of a future, from a park ranger in Kissimmee, Florida. She was humiliated and helpless. She had never worked, had spent thirty-five of her sixty years in a body that was mangled in a car accident, and was completely dependent on her children. Of her seven children, only two had lives stable enough to be of much help to her. Zane, the baby from her first marriage, and Mike, the oldest of her children with Frank, took most of the emotional, physical, and financial responsibility for Mother. The others did what they could. But I was no help. By the time Frank and Sally left, I had already run away with a man I had known for only two months. In the summer of 1982, Frank and I stranded Mother in a single-wide trailer in a fishing camp on Lake Tohopekaliga.

3

THE HOLE THINGS FALL INTO

I spent six years running away from the life that broke open the summer of Frank and Sally—six years, exchanging army bases and campgrounds for the navy bases of married life. Running blind, away from my old life, I ended up recreating it. Lewis was a radiation technician on naval nuclear submarines. His entire psychic life was governed by rules, procedures, drills, training—and the constant, chronic fear of failing. Every action governed by fear and disorientation: Lewis's fear of punishment for any infraction—being late, being unshaved, wearing unironed uniform, falling asleep on watch, forgetting log entries.

Fear and disorientation. The disorientation of shift work—switching back and forth from days to nights, sometimes thirty-six-hour shifts, sometimes twelve on, twelve off. Sleep deprivation, bodies that stopped recognizing the difference between day and night. My life—school, work, any "meaning" I could make—centered on Lewis, when he went to the boat, when he came home, when he was in port, when he was gone. Pressing dress blues for Lewis's inspections on the base, learning how to iron the pants inside-out so the seams would lie flat, how to tie the blue scarf for the dress whites. Packing duffle bags for deployment. Moving from duty station to duty station, moving across a continent and the Pacific Ocean, and seeing, always, only, the minutiae of laundry, of picking up and dropping off, of grocery shopping and making dinner, of alarm clocks going off at all hours of the day and night, never enough sleep, alternating between adrenalin spikes and crashed-out tired. An episodic life, marked by irregular intervals. A life that could never find a steady rhythm.

And always—always—the eruptions of anger that fear and confusion bring. Some trivial thing—any trivial thing—could trigger shame, rage, day after day of me crying, Lewis angry and withdrawn. Sometimes, violence. At first, mostly minor—he would slap me, kick me, once and be done. I would cry. Eventually, the work of forgetting would white out whatever had happened. (But it got worse. Finally, forgetting could not work.)

I left Florida, left the summer of Frank and Sally, vowing that I would never, ever be my mother, never be humiliated, talked down to, treated like dirt. Vowed that I would be strong, respected. And I lived, those years with Lewis, exactly like she did with Frank. Centered around him. Governed by his moods, his actions. Triggering him. And then forgetting. Running away from the summer of Frank and Sally, I re-created the very thing I was fleeing.

Except, not exactly: I managed to stay in school.

I worked school in around Lewis's duty stations: a semester at the Parson's Project Branch of the New School for Social Research in Ballston Spa, New York. The last year and a half of my bachelor's degree at the University of Hawaii in Manoa. My master's degree from the University of California at San Diego. I worked: cashiering at King's Department Store in Glenville, New York; secretarial work at Alexander Brothers in Honolulu; temp agency appointments in San Diego. I got student loans, a graduate fellowship. It is true, I did all this. But this wasn't my "life," my center, the main part of my living—it was the addendum to a life that was defined by drinking-fighting-crying, punctuated by months of separation when Lewis went to sea. I was my mother, living drinking-fighting-crying nights, punctuated by months of separation when her husbands went to war. I was my father, amazed at my own survival, at the superabundance of a life that provided military quarters, military doctors, the guaranty of a roof and a bed in this world of refugees and homelessness. I was the twelve-year-old, escaping into the refuge of school, using books and homework and term papers to drown out the sounds of drinking-fighting-crying.

In the six years that I spent running from the summer of Frank and Sally, I couldn't look back. I couldn't even stop and take a good look at the here and now. I stared fiercely into the "future," running toward what I thought would be "better."

Frank,

> Was it like this for you too? An adolescent running blind, carrying a past you couldn't escape into a future you hoped would be better? How old were you when you went into the army? When you married Mother, a woman five years older than you with three young daughters?
>
> Were you lost and alone in the world, clinging to the hope that, with Mother, "survival" was possible?
>
> Were you stumbling around under the weight of your ghosts, fearful, angry, crying, longing, yearning, hoping?
>
> Did you lose yourself in the drama of the drinking-fighting-crying so that you wouldn't have to look at the ghosts sitting on your shoulders, directing your actions?
>
> I ran away with the first man who took pity on me, who offered me a way out of the summer of you and Sally. And isn't this something like what you did when you first ran to the army?
>
> All that work I did to forget, and I just repeated the things I was fleeing, repeated the history of your forgetting. Is this the way forgetting works? Does it demand that we repeat the pasts we refuse to witness?
>
> At eighteen, how could I have known that I was recreating your trajectory?
>
> What trajectories were you recreating?

I grew up with the story that Frank lied about his age and enlisted in the army when he was seventeen, at the tail end of World War II. On my birth certificate, Frank's birth date is given as October 24, 1926, and the date of his first enlistment as 1948. This paper makes Frank twenty-two years old when he enlisted, three years after the war was over, twenty-five when he got out of the army the first time in 1951. But this birth certificate also says that Mother had five live births with Frank. Frank and Mother, however, have only four children—two boys,

Mike and Leonard, and then two girls, Georgia and me. I asked Zane about this fifth child, the ghost listed on my birth certificate. Zane said, no, that couldn't be. Mother had miscarried once, yes, but Mother and Frank had only four children. So these five live births, Frank's age . . . what are we to believe?

These documents we look to for "proof" of what is "true" turn out to be as fallible as our memories.

But, still—1948? Three years after the end of World War II? I have to presume a truth in this date, that the army got this piece of the paperwork right. A lot depends on this; it marks him as a G.I.— "government issue," property of the U.S. Army. It is the beginning of his military career, and everything about his life as a "soldier" follows from it—pensions, medical benefits, rank. If this date is right, then the stories I was told are wrong.

Whatever the case with his first enlistment, all the stories agree that, after he got out of the army, Frank went back to his home town of Groton, Massachusetts, and took a job in the local paper mill. There, he met and married my mother, a widow with three young daughters. Shortly after they married, Lily, my mother's mother, discovered that Frank was molesting Mother's oldest daughter, Margaret. Lily reported Frank to the police. An investigation followed, after which Frank went back into the army. He did two tours of duty in Korea, one in Vietnam, and in between he and Mother had four more children. I was the last of seven. After Vietnam, he came back to Fort Benjamin Harrison, in Indianapolis—to his wife and the four children still living at home— and requested a transfer to Fort Greely, Alaska. Alaska was our last duty station. Frank retired from the army in the early seventies and spent the next decade working in state parks in south and central Florida. We moved every year or two until I started high school, when we more or less settled at Southport Park, a fish camp that my father ran in Kissimmee, Florida. Finally, in September 1982, Frank left with Sally.

I don't remember anything about Frank before he left for Vietnam —my first memory is of his return and learning what "tan" meant. He was brown from his toes to his thighs and from his head to his belt-line. In between, there was a scary white strip. His two different colors shaped me.

When I first began turning back to confront the effects of Frank in my life, I went back to meet and fight that part of him that it is easy to call "villain." I had to untangle impossible contradictions: Frank "loved" me and gave me preferential treatment. As long as I was Daddy's little girl, obedient, dependent. As long as I was a magic mirror that showed him the image of himself he was seeking. As long as I fed the fantasy of man, daddy, soldier—the images that propped him up and held him together. But he was cruel to Georgia and Mike. They showed their hurt, their anger. They fought against the suffocating embrace of a "love" that would use them as objects, as props in the fantasy of himself that he was acting out. He shamed them. Humiliated them. Beat them.

Once, when I was talking to Mike about the different treatment we received, Mike said, "We all suffered our particular hells at his hands. Mine was beating after beating." Until he was fifteen. Until something broke inside of him. Maybe the last hope he held out for his father's love? And Mike said, finally, "If you ever hit me again, I will kill you. Sooner or later, you will go to sleep and I will kill you." After that, Mike says, Frank left him alone.

What does it take to make a fifteen-year-old boy stand up like that to the man from whom he most needed love? And what does it mean for the "love" Frank kept from Mike and Georgia to have been given to me? How do I trace the threads of Frank's violence, his tenderness, the complicated mixed-up-itness of his incest?

A strand of the "love" Frank gave me: I am seven, eight, nine years old. Sick, again, with strep throat. It is winter, late, dark. At the marina, the campers have set up their folding chairs, ice chests, bait buckets, prepared to fish through the night for bluegill and speckled perch. Frank wraps me in his gray wool army blanket, holds me close to him, carries me with him to join the campers, maybe fish a little. The wool scratches my skin, makes me itch. My throat is on fire. But there is comfort here, wrapped up against the night, my head on my father's chest. On the nights when I am not sick, I join my father as his "helper." Daddy's darling girl, I bait hooks, refill ice and beer supplies, watch for bobbers being snatched under water.

Frank's violence is a chameleon thing. Where in this jumbled bag of "Frank" do I locate the violence of an incest that is wrapped up in an army blanket and fishing for bream while admiring onlookers tell me how lucky I am?

I was afraid of Frank. Afraid of his unpredictable tantrums, afraid of his hurt feelings, afraid of the man he turned into when he was drinking. I was afraid of his yelling, afraid of his guns, afraid of doing something to trigger him. But this was a fear mixed up with guilt, with the feeling that I was failing my father, not loving him enough. A fear that made what I was afraid of my fault. Like everything else I inherited from Frank, my fear was complicated by other emotions that were just its opposite. The fear I had of Frank can't account for the aching-heart quality of some of the memories I have of him. After all these years of trying to understand my father, the images that come to me now are images of Frank planting trees in the campgrounds he worked in, lovingly watering his seedlings. Of Frank sorting through his fishing gear, separating lines by pound and tess, organizing sinkers and bobbers and shiny fly-fishing hooks. Frank coming home with presents— a folding rocking chair he got me at an auction once, books he thought I might want to read.

My rocking chair, my books, exist side by side with Frank's other presents: slinky pajama sets, with wraparound tops trimmed with lace, tenuously fastened with a single metal snap. Sexy bras and underwear. Frank bought Mother's clothes too—discount-rack polyester pantsuits, an occasional caftan. Cheap, ugly chothes for my mother, pretty sexy things for me.

> *This is true. There were "pretty sexy things" for me, but not many. Most of what I wore my mother made me. Other things came from department store preschool sales, when Frank would take Georgia and me shopping and let us pick out a set of school clothes. But, few and far between as they were, the things Frank did buy me—the occasional book, that auction rocking chair, the sexy underwear—marked me.*

I was the baby, Frank's favorite. By the time I was twelve, my older brothers and sisters had all moved away. My sister, Georgia, was the last to leave. Frank did not bring her presents. He followed her, spied on her, made public scenes when he found her talking to boys—at a

Frank holding me as a baby.

school dance, at a summer science camp, in the campgrounds where we lived. He humiliated and shamed her. Cheap, ugly clothes for Mother. Humiliation and shame for Georgia. Pretty sexy things for me. Until the summer of Frank and Sally, this is how I lived, my version of "normal" in the only life I knew.

In retrospect, from the outside, it's easy to say:

"This is wrong! Stop it! Speak up! Leave!"

"Tell somebody."

"Get out of that house."

"Call the police."

From the inside, things weren't so easy.

On the inside, there are secrets and silences, lies, half-truths passing themselves off as the real thing. And ghosts. All the ghosts of the people and things we have run away from, left behind, failed to confront. Ghosts we don't even know, hanging on for generations. The ghost child on my birth certificate. The ghosts Frank carried with him.

Those six years I spent with Lewis, trying to run away, were ruled by my ghosts. My ghosts were spectacular haunters. They came at night, crying my guilt for abandoning Mother, for lying to her about Frank and Sally, for hating her for not being stronger. They were in my silences, the stories about "family" that I could not tell. They were my constant company, the presences that stood between me and my classmates. They demanded all my attention, kept me isolated with them. They were my day-to-day reality, amplified because I could not see them.

4

FORGETTING AND
RE-MEMBERING

I am haunted by things that happened before I was born, histories that are only partly my own. The ghosts hugging me cross genera-tions, collapse time and space; they hold hands with my father, have their fingers threaded through my mother's hair, are locked elbow-to-elbow with my brothers and sisters. Ghosts hid like crumbs in the seams of our car's upholstery. When nobody is sitting down, the seams fold around crumbs too small to see. But, when the weight of a body presses the seams apart, the crumbs stick to sweaty thighs, grind into flesh, make you itch. All those years in the cars taking us from one tem-porary base camp to another, my family's ghosts were like that: itchy grindy things I could not see, working their way into my skin through the open pores of thighs stuck to the back seat.

After six years of moving from navy base to navy base with Lewis, trying to forget Frank and, in the process, re-creating life with him, I moved back to Florida, where my family's ghosts were waiting for me. In May 1988, when my best friend, Denise, and I were visiting my mother, all those ghosts busted through the walls of my forgetting.

In May 1988, Denise and I went back to Davenport, Florida, to visit my mother. I was angry. I was angry that Mother and Frank were still married but that she didn't know where he was. He kept his whereabouts secret from everybody except for my oldest brother Mike. Periodically, Frank sent Mike a small amount of money to help support Mother. Every month, whether Frank sent it or not, Mike deposited the $278 that was supposed to come from Frank into Mother's checking account. I was angry at Mike for keeping the secret of Frank's whereabouts. I was furious with this structure, which I thought infantilized Mother, kept her dependent on her children, prevented her from living with any dignity or self-worth. I thought Mike was helping Frank humiliate Mother.

Mike was angry with me. He thought I was young, naïve, selfish. He believed he was protecting Mother. In fits of rage, Frank had threatened to kill her. Mike believed that he was acting as a buffer between Frank's rage and Mother's vulnerability. I wanted Mother to get a divorce, to have a court-ordered allotment from Frank's military pension deposited directly into her account. I didn't want Mother to be dependent on her children. I wanted her to be strong, in control of her life. (I wanted to be strong, in control of my life.) I was furious with Mother's poverty, furious at the fear that kept all of us in Frank's power. I didn't want him to have power over her anymore. (I didn't want him to have power over me anymore.)

I was angry and guilty. I carried my guilt like a baby, in the pit of my stomach, flinching when its kicking stretched my skin, crumbled my spine. My guilt fed off what I did and did not know: The summer Frank and Sally were having their affair, I knew what they were doing. I'd been keeping secrets for my father my whole life, from army base to army base while I was a child, from campground to campground after he retired. When Frank and Sally told me they were in love, this confidence folded seamlessly into the fabric of a life woven with Frank's secrets. I didn't know how to tell Mother—even when she was suspicious, even when she asked me about it. At eighteen, I didn't know any more about how to protect my mother than I did when I was a child, keeping Frank's secrets for him. The summer of Frank and Sally, I didn't know how to do anything except try to save myself, and my hard, tight fist of anger rises up out of the thick mucus of this guilt.

After six years of piecing together a college education, I brought my anger and my guilt back to Florida with me, where I'd taken a job teaching high school English, had hired a lawyer, and was trying to convince Mother to file for divorce.

A View from the Corner of the Ceiling

When Mother tells the story, again, about how Frank left, my balled-up fist of anger drips with this guilt that feeds it. My guilt and my anger distract me. Mother is telling Denise and me about how afraid she was, how humiliated. She is living now in a large field surrounded by orange groves, with several other mobile homes scattered around her; she pays $75 a month for the lot on which this falling-apart trailer is parked. That leaves her just over $200 a month for the rest of her expenses— food, insurance, electricity, gas. It's not enough. Zane and Mike give her what money they can spare. I haven't given her much.

The more we talk about my mother's poverty, the more agitated I become. My mind begins to wander. It feels strange to be back in this place after six years away from it. This poverty makes me squeamish. I had managed to forget how tenuous a "home" this tin box is. Each year took me farther and farther away from this cut-and-paste house trailer with its small sink and rotting floors, the leaks in the water-stained roof, its sense of impending collapse. Now that I have moved back to Florida, now that I am visiting my mother, I have to remember that this place exists, that this is where I used to live. The kitchen sink seems so small. I remember the meals I cooked there, in that tiny little space with no counters and a stove with its broiler-door fallen off and two of the burner knobs stuck. I cannot imagine how there was room for the endless stream of fish-camp guests we used to host, their dirty cake plates and coffee cups.

I focus my attention, again, on my mother, on Denise, on the cracking gray vinyl of the kitchen chairs and the butcher-block table under my elbows. We are still talking about Frank, about all the terrible things he did, about how he has shamed my mother. We talk about things I never knew before, things that were not allowed to be said while Frank was still here. Mother tells me that she met Frank shortly after her first husband died. Her house was paid off, and she was receiving survivor's benefits from her first husband, who fought in World War II. She also received Social Security benefits for her three small daughters, my half-sisters Margaret, Bernie, and Zane. Mother tells me that Frank used the girls' Social Security money to buy a boat and guns, paid for hunting and fishing trips with his friends. But the girls, she says, had to go to school in old shoes, and there was never enough money to buy them clothes.

The money makes my head spin. Sally divorced her husband, who was rich, and Frank and Sally are living on her divorce settlement. They have a lot of money. But Mother has less than $300 a month, supplemented by money from her children. My anger and agitation increase; I want to find Frank, to hold him responsible, to make him pay. Mother tells Denise and me that Frank has always been like this—greedy, selfish. She gets up and goes to her desk, where she gathers together old, canceled checks—twenty years' worth of money that her mother, Lily, had given to Frank. The checks span the years 1959 to 1974. My head spins faster, my agitation and anger make my blood rush, pound. I become obsessed with counting the checks. I have to put them in order, to find some meaning that I feel hides inside these documents.

I count, over and over again, the money these checks represent; $3,000 for the years 1965, 1966, and 1967 is recorded in these checks. The money I am counting is from the years after I was born, some of it money Frank received when we lived in Germany, some from when Frank was in Vietnam. I remember Frank coming home from Vietnam. We were living in a trailer on an army base in Fort Benjamin Harrison, in Indianapolis. How old was I? Four or five? This is where I have my first memory of my father, coming home from Vietnam two different colors. He was brown from his toes to his thighs and then from his beltline to his head. In between, there was a scary white strip.

I grow more agitated, count the checks over and over. Looking at these checks, at the $3,000 Lily gave Frank in the years 1965, 1966, and 1967, I begin to be afraid. I remember Frank, just back from Vietnam, lean and brown except for the white strip of flesh where his shorts should have been. I remember being small, in a room with this brown-skinned man with the scary white strip, and repeating words from the television commercial for the toothpaste we used: "I brushed with Ultrabrite, so I have sex appeal."

These checks, this time that is a blank space for me, begin to terrify me. Who has kept these checks, and why? Why did my grandmother give Frank all this money? Why did she keep the canceled checks all these years? Why, after Lily died, did Mother keep these documents?

Sitting with my elbows on the table and concentration fixed fiercely on these checks, I begin sinking, sliding beneath a fear that is engulfing me. Something is going to get me, to hurt me. I feel as though I am in a huge, haunted house, being led down dark and cobwebbed hallways to stand, terrified, in front of doors that I do not want to open. Monsters crouch behind those doors, waiting to get me, to pounce on me and devour me, to hurt me if I go through them.

While I am sliding beneath this terror, a calm, watching part of me sees my mother, Denise, the table, coffee cups. I get up, thinking that I cannot hurt my mother—I have an urgent desire to protect her from this feeling overcoming me. I go into my old bedroom and sit. A crying comes upon me, a crying that seems to be both something I am doing and something I am watching. I am split, divided into two beings: one who is afraid of the monsters in the haunted house, crying, unable to stop, and one who watches my frightened, crying self like one watches a play being performed. The frightened, crying me is sitting on my bed, while the watching me is in the corner of the ceiling, by the bathroom, looking down.

The looking-down, watching me says, "NO! STOP! You can't do this, you have to stop crying." This part of me says, "You can't hurt Mother. You have to protect her. Don't hurt Mother."

This part of me who is careful about my mother watches the me who is crying, shaking, trembling. A part of me is lost, terrified, out of control, held within another part that is defined, contained, controlling.

Finally, my split selves come together. The part of me watching and saying, "NO! You cannot do this" gets the part of me crying to stand up, scrub at my tears, go back to the kitchen.

When I sit back down at the table, with the cups and the checks and my mother and Denise, the crying self is contained, quiet. I am calm, detached, outside myself. From this outside myself place, I say that I feel as though I am in a haunted house. I do not mention crying, although I wonder if they heard me. Surely they must have heard me— the trailer is so small, the walls so thin, you can hear a person peeing no matter where in the trailer you are sitting. I watch my mother, looking for some sign that she has heard me. Denise looks at me, bewildered. My mother changes the subject.

I feel, for the rest of the hour that Denise and I stay in that kitchen, at that table with my mother, that I have been dreaming. I feel that half-conscious feeling that comes between the buzzing of time-delayed alarms. I do not remember what we talk about after the haunted house. Time has folded in on me, suspending me in an in-between. Finally, Denise and I leave.

Outside, I can breathe again. I realize, as my lungs expand with gulps of the damp night air, that I had been holding my breath. It is so dark that we can barely see the car, but I am comforted by this blackness. The haunted-house fog that has clouded me begins to lift, my head begins to clear. I get into Denise's car, anxious to move back into the safe place of this friendship. Denise was my first friend in Kissimmee, the only friend I have kept from my high school days. We weathered adolescence together, college, our first professional jobs. Most important, we imagined our futures. Together, we struggled to find meaning in our lives, to discover what we wanted from work, relationships, the day-to-day lives that we could make. I want this friendship to pull me out of the in-between of time folding in on me, to bring me back to the Lori who teaches high school, dreams of her Ph.D.

But Denise does not let my crying go. She asks, "What happened in there?"

I spent my college years dissecting literature, asking, "Why?" and "What does it mean?" of everything. I have a job teaching English to high school students, and I demand that they look below the surface of the things we read, look deep to find meaning. But now, tonight, I do not want to know why, do not want answers, do not want to explain this thing. I do not know what has happened, what it means. I do not want to know. I want to lose myself in the darkness of this night, in the smell of damp earth and vegetation and the sounds of insects and frogs. I do not want to remember the cramped trailer, the smells and sounds of people crowding me, the tin walls suffocating me.

Denise pulls out of the driveway, confused, not sure what she has just witnessed. She is a software engineer, and she wants to know why, how—how things fit together, how to fix them. She wants to make sense of this night. She asks me questions. Why did I go into my old bedroom? Why was I crying? Why did I come back to the kitchen table and continue drinking my coffee as though nothing had happened? What did I mean by a haunted house? Why didn't my mother want to talk about it? How could she just change the subject? Why did I go along with it? What *happened* in there? Denise is urgent, determined. I am like one of her programs that will not run: I have a bug somewhere, something wrong, and she will locate the problem and fix it. She is tenacious, reliable, strong.

"I don't know." I am still scared, confused. I do not have words to explain what I do not understand myself.

I remember something Zane told me last winter.

"Before we left California, Zane told me that Frank had gone to trial for something, a long time ago. She was vague, didn't say what, exactly—but she thought it might have been for raping somebody. But she told me not to say anything and not to ask Mother about it. She said Mother doesn't like to talk about it."

"Then you have to call Zane." Denise is resolute. She pulls back onto the road.

What do we remember, and what do we forget? Like with shooting—I know I am a good shot. I can't draw a straight line, play a video game, or do practically anything that requires hand-eye coordination, but I can shoot a gun. I clearly remember hour after hour of target practice behind the retention ponds at Southport Park, just me and my favorite .22 rifle. But I cannot muster a single memory of learning how to shoot. I cannot say how I learned to load a rifle, how to stand with my body at an angle and my left foot forward. How to nuzzle the butt just so between my shoulder and my cheek. The difference between aiming with a scope and aiming through the sight at the end of the barrel. I couldn't tell you how I learned to let my body go backward with the kick of a shotgun, or how it is that, during my one and only try at skeet shooting, I hit my second target while all the gun-knowing men shooting with me missed disc after disc. I can't even remember Frank's guns. I know he had a .45, .22s, shotguns, and cases full of rifles. I know I shot many of them. But my memory of these guns is fragmented, discontinuous.

My brother Mike told me, "You have been shooting since you were six years old."

Like all my memories of Frank's violence, this slippery memory leaves a lot unaccounted for.

Forgetting Is Like This

I am twelve years old, maybe eleven, and Frank has thrown my mother and my sister out of the house. It is around Thanksgiving. I am sitting on the sofa, next to Frank. The sofa is black vinyl, and I am concentrating hard on the two black horse-shaped lamps in the living room. Mother and Georgia are outside, locked out, and Frank is telling me things. He is serious, stares hard at me. I do not want him to know that I do not understand what he is saying. Words are coming out of his mouth, but they do not mean anything to me; I cannot remember them. I nod, say things—what do I say? I am afraid that he will find out that I cannot hear what he is saying. Somehow, an ambulance comes—I think it is an ambulance, but maybe it is the police? Some kind of car with sirens. Frank refuses to get in this siren-vehicle, sends it away.

These fragments—that there is a night when my father throws my mother and sister out of the house, that it is around Thanksgiving when I am eleven or twelve, that I am sitting on a black vinyl sofa in the living room of our trailer, staring at black horse-shaped lamps and afraid that my father will find out that I am not listening to what he is saying to me—this is all I am sure of.

Re-membering Is Like This

Many years later, when we are both adults, I ask my sister Georgia if she remembers a night when Frank threw her and Mother out of the house, when a siren-vehicle came and Frank refused to get in it. She says yes, she remembers. Frank was mad at her again. She cannot remember why; he was always yelling, always mad at her for something. She remembers Frank telling her to leave, to get out of the house. Mother protesting. Frank telling Mother she can leave too—get the Hell out of there. She remembers Mother and her, locked out of the trailer, and Mother blaming her for upsetting Frank again. She remembers Frank on a picnic table by our trailer, with a gun. She is not sure who he was going to shoot, but she thinks maybe he was going to shoot himself. She cannot believe I do not remember the gun, that there was going to be this shooting. She remembers an ambulance.

"How did it get there?" I ask her.

"You called it," she says.

I do not remember calling an ambulance. Georgia says I have to have called it—our trailer was in the back of the campground; it was winter; nobody else was around. I was the only one allowed inside, the only one who could have gotten to a phone.

I do not remember calling an ambulance, and I do not remember Frank's gun.

I work up the courage to ask Mother what she remembers about this night.

"Hey, Mom?" I try to be gentle. Over the years of my re-membering, Mother has grown suspicious of my questions. They stick her, make her bleed. She has to protect herself from me.

"Yes, baby?"

"Mom, do you remember a night, in Okeechobee, around Thanksgiving, when Frank threw you and Georgia out of the house?"

Mother gets upset, starts to shake. Her nerves are not up to my questions today. "I don't want to talk about this," she says.

"Okay," I say. I let it go. Today, I do not want to be the knife cutting into her.

This is how forgetting and re-membering work.

INTERLUDE I

On the Event without a Witness

People ask me about Frank, "What happened?"

What happened is the haunted house and my nightmares and the skin shudders and then calling my sisters. What happened is birth to age eighteen living inside incomprehensible cycles of drinking, fighting, yelling, crying, hurting, longing. What happened is the chronic work of forgetting helped along by alarm clocks and work and school and getting dinner ready. What happened is Frank and Sally and then six years of running away from the incomprehensible mess trailing me.

In psychoanalytic terms, I had to go back and encounter a past that had remained unencountered. To go back and encounter the past is not so much a matter of pinning down details of events that we can never really "recover" as it is understanding the effects of the past on our lives so that we can imagine a future—a future beyond old wounds, old fears, old angers, and old resentments. These concepts—the possibility that a past can remain unencountered and unwitnessed, and that surviving beyond trauma requires turning back to pasts that we must encounter and to which we must bear witness—have shaped the way I think about living.

But what does it mean for a past to be unencountered?

I have come to think about this idea in two ways. The first is through my amateur forays into feminist psychoanalytic theory. The second is through my even more amateurish readings of lay accounts of neuroscience.

Cathy Caruth, a literary theorist, writes in *Unclaimed Experience: Trauma, Narrative, and History:* "Trauma is not locatable in the simple violent or original event in an individual's past, but rather in the way that its very unassimilated nature—the way it was precisely *not known* in the first instance—returns to haunt the survivor later on" (1996, 4). There is a "complex relation between knowing and not knowing" (3), and the "truth" of trauma is not simply a matter of what is known; it is linked "also to what remains unknown in our very actions and our language" (4).

This idea that there is something that is *not known* in our actions and our language is borne out by recent work in the field of neuroscience. Eric R. Kandel, a neuroscientist who won the 2000 Nobel Prize in Physiology or Medicine for his research on the physiological basis of memory storage in neurons, says that science has "validated Freud's theory that the majority of our actions are unconscious" (2007, 133). While science cannot explain "the hard problem of consciousness— the mystery of how neural activity gives rise to subjective experience" (382), research on the molecular and biological workings of emotion has identified that there are both conscious and unconscious components of emotion, and these involve different areas of the brain and different neural activity. "The conscious component of emotion . . . involves the evaluative functions of the cerebral cortex, which are carried out by the cingulate cortex" (342). Unconscious emotion, however, involves the "autonomic nervous system and the hypothalamus, which regulates it" (342). The neural systems that "store unconscious, implicit, emotionally charged memories" are *different* from those that generate the memory of conscious, explicit feeling states.[1]

These unconscious components of emotion are especially important factors in fear. The amygdala, a part of the brain deep inside the cortex, mediates fear (Kandel 2007, 45, 387). When fear is conscious, the dorsal region of the amygdala is activated. When fear is unconscious, however, the basolateral nucleus of the amygdala is activated.

---

1 For a more detailed account of the science I have summarized here, see particularly the chapters "The Brain's Picture of the External World," "Attention Must Be Paid," and "Mice, Men, and Mental Illness" in Kandel 2007. See also Damasio 2003.

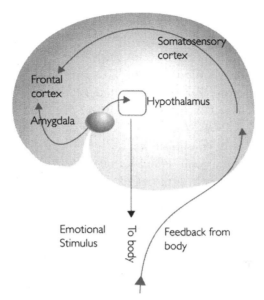

Emotional stimuli are registered by the amygdala. Conscious emotion is created both by direct signals from the amygdala to the frontal cortex and indirectly. The indirect path involves the hypothalamus, which sends hormonal messages to the body to create physical changes like muscle contraction, heightened blood pressure, and increased heart rate. These changes are then fed back to the somatosensory cortex, which feeds the information forward to the frontal cortex, where it is interpreted as emotion.

(Illustration/caption from Rita Carter, *Mapping the Mind* [Berkeley: University of California Press, 1999], p. 82. Used with permission from University of California Press.)

The basolateral nucleus of the amygdala "receives most of the incoming sensory information and is the primary means by which the amygdala communicates with the cortex" (Kandel 2007, 387).

The amygdala sends the "sensory information" in the fear-provoking environment to the cortex—a father yelling, a body hit or "touched," a sister crying, a gun going off. Other sensory information is communicated too—the smell in the room, the way a man snaps his fingers to make you crawl like a dog. These neutral stimuli can become associated with what we are afraid of. Furthermore, the amygdala can "retain the memory of [a] threat throughout an organism's entire life" (Kandel 2007, 343). This is what scientists call "learned fear." In this way, "neutral stimuli" can become "powerful triggers of long-term emotional memories in people" (Kandel 2007, 342). The fireworks on the Fourth of July that send combat veterans diving for cover. The sounds from a love scene on television that make a teenager feel nauseated. Throughout our entire lives, unconscious fears may trigger the physical, emotional, and psychological states of a past trauma. This learned fear is "a key component" of many psychiatric disorders (Kandel 2007, 342).

Research in neuroscience gives a different weight to Caruth's argument that "trauma is not locatable in the simple violent or original event in an individual's past, but rather in the way that its very unassimilated nature—the way it was precisely *not known* in the first instance—returns to haunt the survivor later on" (1996, 4). Here, psychoanalysis and neuroscience seem to agree: Trauma is "the unwitting reenactment of an event that one cannot simply leave behind" (2).

If we cannot simply leave our trauma behind, neither can we simply return to the original trauma, confront it, and be done with it. If memory has both conscious and unconscious components, how do we turn back to what is unconscious in us? How do we decipher the neuro-chemical-biological messages triggering our fear, anger, shame, keeping us trapped inside emotions and patterns that are destructive to ourselves and others? Again, neuroscience and psychoanalysis agree: "Most of our mental life is unconscious; it becomes conscious only as words and images" (Kandel 2007, 424). The process of return, then, is a process of bringing what is unconscious into language.

But how do we do this?

Kandel argues that one of the crucial questions neuroscience has still to unravel is "how the unconscious processing of sensory information occurs and how conscious attention guides the mechanisms in the brain that stabilize memory" (2007, 424). We need to pause here, to go slowly with these words:

- "unconscious processing of sensory information"
- "conscious attention"
- "the mechanisms in the brain that stabilize memory"

What is the "unconscious processing of sensory information" for the sounds coming from another room in the middle of the night? Loud thumping sounds—something is being hit. What? A body? Who? Where? The living room? Your brothers' bedroom? Shouting, banging. Protests—Mother's voice, maybe? Cabinets slamming, things breaking. Dishes? In the kitchen? Knickknacks? Where is Georgia? Crying. A long period of silence. Holding breath, waiting. Trying both to hear and to not hear, to know and to not know.

What is it, of a night like this, that is remembered? Some things can be known—the crying, the yelling, the hitting, the banging, the breaking. Some things cannot be known—who, what, where, why. What is stored consciously, and what remains unconscious?

"Conscious attention" is a matter of language—it is the words we give to a scene, the sense we make of it. It is the interpretation we make, the understanding we reach. To "stabilize memory" is to be able to tell a story: "On February 2, 1969, Frank came home at three o'clock in the morning, drunk, after an unannounced white-glove inspection at the base. Repeating this inspection at home, he found a fork that was not quite 'clean.' In a rage, he entered his daughters' bedroom, grabbed Georgia by the hair, dragged her into the kitchen, pulled all the dishes out of the cabinets, threw many of them, broke some, and made her wash every dish in the house. While Georgia was washing dishes and picking up strewn flatware, Frank was yelling at her—pig, slut, irresponsible, ungrateful, filthy, dirty little whore."

To tell a story is to locate an event, pin it down. To place an event in a logical order of time. To make it fit a pattern, a view of the world. But some events cannot be pinned down like that. What does "February 2, 1969" mean to a child of five? When it is just one of a hundred such nights? When you cannot quite make out all the words that are being yelled or be sure what is being banged around? Where is the "conscious attention that stabilizes memory" in the tension of a body straining to both know and not know, to both hear and not hear, the sounds coming from another room? How does the unconscious process the sensory information from a childhood of being woken in the middle of the night, the sounds of shouting, hitting, crying? Where do the body's memories live—the sound of the bedroom door opening, the smell of gin, the red glow of a cigarette that, for the rest of your life, can make you hold your breath?

5

RE-MEMBERING II

It seems to me now that, when Zane hinted at the trial, she was trying to tell me about Frank, to ask me if anything had happened to me. But she couldn't do it directly. We had to go slowly, circling the edges of the pasts we'd been living as secrets. Encounter the shock of what our sideways looking revealed and then fall back, regroup, and readjust. Get up and start tracing, again, the secret center of our family. Our re-membering was a spiral dance, a complicated tapping between the here-and-now and the there-and-then.

The night the haunted house opened up and started spilling out our family's ghosts, Denise changed everything. She was my first witness. She stood firm against the years of forgetting, against the desire to round up the escaping ghosts and lock them away again. When I awoke the next day at Denise's apartment, I was disoriented, confused, feeling that I was in the grip of an undertow pulling me into the deep of the ocean. I was shaking, heart palpitating, head caving under a pressure that left me dizzy. All I wanted was for these pains in my body to go away. I was ashamed, guilty, embarrassed. I was afraid I was going crazy. I was afraid for my job—if people knew what my body was doing, would they fire me? Lock me up in a crazy-people's place?

Denise planted her feet, resolute, unrelenting, and looked straight into this crazy.

Skin Shudders

Denise makes coffee. She is still shaken. Last night changed things; "things" are not "normal" anymore. This is different from when we were eighteen and Frank and Sally were having an affair. Then, "they" were "fucked up"—it was not me who was crying and screaming and making no sense. When I called Denise from California and told her Frank and Sally were "in love," I was calm. Crazy things were happening around me, but "I" was not "crazy." Now, the crazy is coming from me.

"Are you okay?" Denise asks.

"Yeah, I'm good," I say.

Our awkward half-laughs say what our words cannot: Of course I am not okay, of course we know this. But we don't know how to say what has happened, how to fix it, how to begin the long, slow work of understanding what this rupture means. We know enough to know we can't go back, but we don't know how to go forward yet.

We drink our coffee, repeat the things from the night before. I say that I will call my sisters when I get home—Zane, Margaret, Bernie, Georgia. Tell them what has happened to me. Ask them what they know. Ask them if they ever felt like they were going crazy before.

Finally, I leave—start the two-hour drive from Orlando to Newberry, where I have to get ready to teach the next day.

After the haunted house, after getting up off Denise's sofa and driving back home, my body endures wave upon wave of what I call my "skin shudders": The skin at the top of my skull contracts and cinches up the rest of the skin down my head, on my neck, across my shoulders, down to the small of my back. Everything stops in my stomach, into which my genitals contract and go into deep freeze. I spend days in an insomniac blur.

Nothing I do stops the skin shudders or shakes the fog out of my head. I drink coffee, take cold showers. I clean everything, obsessively. I exercise until my muscles out-scream the rest of my body. Nothing works.

I become terrified of sleep. When I sleep, I dream. Over and over again, I dream that I am being chased, that somebody is going to get me, to shoot me, to kill me, because I have "told." The sleep I am getting comes in the afternoons, after work, before dark. I still dream, but the terror effect is not as bad if it is still daylight when I wake up.

One afternoon, I am inside a very bad dream when the phone rings. I pull myself out of the dreaming to something like "awake." I have trouble standing, getting to the phone. My head is pounding, my heart is coming out of my chest, and I think I am going to throw up. When I get to the phone, my niece Ann is on the other end. I have to ask her to wait a few minutes before I can talk because of my head and my heart and having to throw up. When I can speak, she asks if I am sick.

"No," I say.

"Just tired?" she asks.

"Yes."

Finally, when the skin shudders will not stop and I find myself locking my classroom door during planning periods and at lunch so that I can cry undisturbed, I decide to call Vicki. Vicki helped me get through the San Diego days, when the drinking-crying-fighting that Lewis and I were re-creating started getting violent. When I didn't know how I could keep waking up every day to continue the work of living. During my lunch break, I drive to a pay phone out of sight of the high school. I do not want anybody to see what I am doing. I call Vicki and tell her what is happening. I describe the night the monsters started tearing down the walls of the haunted house, my little observation nook in the wall-ceiling cranny, my skin shudders. I still have to teach fifth, sixth, and seventh periods today, plus the rest of May and the first week of June, and I do not see how I can do this when my body shrieks and screams, gets dizzy and heavy, fogs up and blacks out, won't let me sleep.

Vicki, over that lifeline connecting her San Diego office to my Florida pay-phone hiding place, says, "You are having anxiety attacks." She tells me to go to a doctor, explain what is happening, ask for Xanax and a recommendation to a good therapist.

Fortunately for me, I found Kathrin. As witness, my therapist, Kathrin, was not simply good—she was extraordinary. In 1988, I had no idea that American psychologists, courts, and media were on the verge of breaking out into bitter fights over the "truth" of "recovered" memories. On the cusp of the memory controversy, I brought the haunted house, my skin shudders, and my nightmares to Kathrin, who taught me how to live through my heart pounding my eyeballs out and my skin crawling away from my bones. She showed me how to sip water through a straw to stop my crying, how to breathe my heart back to a normal rhythm. She taught me to see my body breaking open as a way of letting something that had been held down too long find its way to the surface. Kathrin taught me to celebrate every panic attack, every ghost that comes to find me. Learn how to sit still through the splitting of my body, how to look for the gift this opening is trying to bring me. And she taught me how to live through my nightmares. But first, she taught me how to learn to find a "truth" in my relation to my mother and sisters.

————

When I was able to talk to Margaret about Frank, she told me that he used to take her for drives in the car. These were the times when he would tell her what boys would want to do to her. Then he would show her the things he told her, so "she would know." These were the things she should not let boys do.

Margaret talks slowly, with many pauses. Like she is dredging words up out of a subterranean cavern. Sentences, subjects and verbs, a few connecting words. No adjectives. Stripped to their bare minimum.

"What happened after Lily told the police?"

"Frank went to trial, and he was acquitted."

"Acquitted?"

"Yes."

"Then what?"

"Then he went back in the army."

"Why didn't anybody ever tell me?"

"I swore a vow of silence."

"A vow of silence?"

"Yes."

"What do you mean?"

"Mother took me to a Catholic church and had me swear a vow of silence. I wasn't allowed to talk about it."

"How old were you?"

"Eleven."

Silence.

Each word the slow, painful lifting of a crushing weight, my questions a digging, an excavation, a blind groping through years and layers of sedimentation.

I tell her about my nightmares, about not being able to sleep. I ask her to tell me what she can remember about Frank.

"Frank was nice to me."

"Nice?"

"Yes."

"How?"

"He would take me places, buy me ice cream. He said this was our special time together, our secret. And he didn't hit Mother."

"Who hit Mother?"

"My father. Before he died, sometimes they would get drunk and get in fights. He used to hit her. Sometimes it was bad."

"How bad?"

"Well, one time she was bleeding, and I didn't know what to do. There was no 911 then. I was only five or six, and I didn't know how to get help. But she was bleeding, and I didn't know how to stop it."

I didn't know any of the things Margaret was telling me. I knew that she had a different father from mine, but I didn't know anything about him—didn't know his name, how he had died, that he drank and hit Mother.

The story I was finally able to piece together: Mother was eighteen years old, living in her hometown of New Orleans, when she met Patrick O'Brien. They met during World War II: Patrick, in his air force uniform, a could-be hero. Mother was already engaged when she met him, but she fell in love with this hardcore Irish man who loved to laugh and dance, who "knew how to have a good time." She and Patrick married shortly after meeting; Patrick shipped out to the Pacific three months after the wedding. Six months later, Margaret was born. By the time she was nineteen, my mother had an infant daughter and a husband at war.

Patrick was gone for three years. When he returned from the war, they transferred to Fort Devens Air Force Base, just outside Boston—near Patrick's family, away from everything Mother had ever known.

They had two more daughters, Bernie and Zane. Patrick, her daughters, air force bases in the years after the Second World War—this was my mother's life from ages twenty-two to twenty-seven. Until the night she was driving Patrick to work in a violent storm and their car wrecked. Patrick died instantly. When the rescue crew arrived, they believed that Mother, the steering wheel and windshield wrapped around her, could not have survived. They got Margaret, Bernie, and Zane out of the back of the car but left Mother where she was. Margaret would not leave her mother, though. At nine years old, insisting that Mother was alive, she waited until a rescue crew cut through folds of metal and retrieved her mother before she would get in the ambulance and go to the hospital.

Mother and the girls survived, but with costs. They spent months in the hospital to repair broken body parts—hips, knees, backs, bones twisted every which way. Mother was the worst. Her jaw was wired shut, and her feet, which the doctors wanted to amputate, became part flesh and bone, part metal hinges and rods.

Mother spent the better part of a year in and out of her hospital home, having surgeries, encased in casts, learning how to use her body again. She fostered her daughters out to friends until her mother, Lily, was able to leave New Orleans and move to Boston to help her. Patrick's family had never liked her—they had disapproved of Patrick's marriage to Mother, and they blamed her for his death. During the hospital days, they weren't much help. When Mother met Frank, she was a widow with three young daughters, estranged from her husband's family, living on survivor's benefits from Patrick's military service, dependent on her mother to help raise her children. This was the scene Frank entered, the context in which he appeared as a "good" husband, a "good" father.

Mother, Margaret, and Zane have different experiences of life after their father died.

According to Margaret: They were happy after Frank came. Margaret remembers being poor when her father was alive. She was only four years old when Patrick and Mother brought Bernie, born three months premature, home. Bernie was so tiny that she slept in a shoe box. Frequently, Mother was unable to get out of bed to take care of Bernie. Margaret remembers Bernie crying for what seemed an interminable time—a tiny dot in that shoe box, throwing up a plea for help. Finally, when Mother did not move, Margaret would muster her

Back, from left to right: *Zane, Bernie.* Front, from left to right: *Georgia, Leonard, Frank, Lori, Dee, Mike.*

four-year-old strength and pick Bernie up, try to feed her, to change her, to figure out what she needed, to take care of her.

> *In retrospect, Margaret thinks Mother was clinically depressed. Mother does not like to talk about that time. She never says that she was "depressed." When I ask her what it was like, she says, simply, "I managed."*

Margaret lived years like this: a child caring for a baby born three months premature, and Patrick sometimes hitting Mother until she bled. So maybe Frank didn't seem so bad by comparison? Patrick drank and hit Mother, but Frank just drank and sometimes "touched" Margaret. And, after the investigation, after Frank went back into the army, the touching stopped. Once a month, somebody from the army came to talk to her, to check on Frank, to make sure that no more "touching" was going on.

According to Zane: They were "well off" until Mother married Frank. The house was paid off, her grandmother was there to take care of her, to give her cookies and cake and sometimes presents. She had friends and family and a neighborhood. After the investigation, Mother sold her house, gave the money to Frank to use, and followed him onto army bases, through two wars and three overseas deployments. They went from settled and stable with enough money to get by on to itinerant army brats living on an enlisted man's salary. From Zane's point of view, Frank ruined everything. Zane, who was only three years old when that car wrecked and her father died, didn't live through Bernie's birth or wonder if she should call the police about her father hitting her mother. After Frank came, she was torn away from her home and her "Grandma Junot" and sent to a school she did not like. From her point of view, they were doing fine until Frank came along: a real house, enough money, a neighborhood, the three girls and Mother. She wished it could have stayed that way.

Where they agree: Mother, Zane, Bernie, and Margaret all agree on certain facts: that the car wreck in which their father died left them all injured, hospitalized for long periods of time. That Lily left New Orleans and came to Massachusetts to help take care of the children. That Frank and Mother met while Mother was still recovering from her body being busted up in every direction. That Margaret told Lily about Frank "fiddling" with her, and Lily reported this to the police. That an investigation occurred, during which the girls went to boarding school. They all remember a "trial" and Frank being "acquitted," then Frank going back into the military.

But they have lived lives colored differently by these events, carrying different meanings.

Mother lived the next twenty-eight years telling herself that Lily was "meddling," Frank was innocent, he was "acquitted."

Margaret lived crushed, silenced, shamed first by being asked to tell and then again by not being believed.

Zane lived pissed, angry that her life was "good" until Frank came along and fucked it up.

The irony here: All these years later, it is Margaret who thinks Frank tried to be a "good" father. Shame and humiliation lived side by side with something like gratitude. On the one hand, she has her twelve-year-old's memory of a courtroom, of Frank smirking when the judge asked him if he "did it"—Frank, smirking and sarcastic, saying, "If she says so, I must have." On the other hand, she holds the memory of Mother so depressed she could not get out of bed, bathe, attend to personal hygiene. When Frank came, he helped take care of the younger children, made Mother get out of bed, take a bath, get dressed. She remembers Frank working two jobs to support them. All these years later, she holds this idea of Frank as a "good" father together with the police, a trial, a judge, people asking her questions and making her repeat herself over and over again, only to be, in the end, shamed, silenced.

Piecing this story together, from a distance of forty years, shows the "truth" to be an elusive thing. My amateur foray into historical records failed to locate evidence of a criminal trial against Frank in 1954. Without a trial, no "acquittal" could occur. So what exactly is it that Margaret, Bernie, Zane, and Mother remember? To find out the "truth" of what happened according to the legal system, I could perhaps search old police reports, newspapers, whatever remains of the files kept by social services agencies. But truths exist that our laws cannot account for—emotional truths. The effects on us of things we have lived but not fully understood. The meanings we give to events. For Margaret, Bernie, Zane, and Mother, "Frank" meant something different. Each of these meanings, in their differences and their contradictions, follows an emotional logic, has a "truth" to tell.

Like this: Margaret remembers Mother taking her to a Catholic church and having her swear a vow of silence. After this, she started to doubt herself—maybe she was crazy? Maybe she imagined it, dreamed it, made it all up? Mother, however, denies imposing this vow of silence. But she denied it to me, forty years after the fact, when I was accusing, angry, blaming her. If Margaret had brought this up with Mother—had asked, for instance, about a day in church when Mother told her not to talk about the trial anymore—would her memory have been different? Or this: Next to Margaret's doubt is Bernie's memory—she remembers Frank taking her for rides and masturbating while he was driving. How do we define the difference between the sexual transgression Bernie remembers and the touching that made Lily call the police? Between a "private" family dysfunction and a "crime" that can be prosecuted?

How do we assign meaning to our experiences, and how do the meanings we assign shape the rest of our perceptions, our actions, our relations?

How, too, is "remembering" an event shaped by its context? The timing of a question, the tone in a voice, the feeling of safety or threat—these things all affect what we remember and how we remember it. Some contexts open up a space for remembering. A soft voice, empathy, compassion—these can draw our memories out of hiding. Some contexts scare our memories away. Me, angry and accusing, Mother denying.

The "truth" is as much the complicated relation between the time, the place, and the context of our remembering as it is the "facts" we might find in records fifty years old.

A truth: lives bent by the weight of secrets too heavy to carry, hearts constricted by the silences we could not break. For more than thirty years, Margaret, Bernie, Zane, and Mother did not speak openly of these events. They lived their memories as secret things they were forbidden to speak.

I inherited this silence.

INTERLUDE II

On Bearing Witness

Fear and shame lived in my family, deep inside our bodies, deep inside our psyches. Governing every feeling, thought, action. Every relation. A primal thing. Teresa Brennan in *The Transmission of Affect* argues that the evolutionary task in front of us is to learn how to connect our conscious world to our unconscious bodily processes. To trace, for example, how we think and act to the force our emotions exert on us. It is a task for which we are, at present, vastly underequipped. As Brennan puts it, "We only have a rudimentary language for connecting sensations, affects, and words, for connecting bodily processes and the conceptual understanding of them. The development of that language requires an attention to the pathways of sensation in the body, an attention that is more concentrated and sustained than the attention received by the body hitherto" (2004, 153). To develop the new vocabulary we need, she says, we must turn into the body.

To turn into the body is to turn into emotion. In accord with such neuroscientists as Antonio Damasio and such psychoanalysts as Arnold Modell, Brennan distinguishes between "emotion" and "feeling." Emotion—or, in Brennan's term, "affect"—is the body's physiological first response to events, objects, thoughts. They are "part of the basic mechanisms of life regulation" (Damasio 2003, 28). Emotions begin with the core of life itself: metabolic regulation, basic reflexes, immune responses, reactions of approach or withdrawal, appetites, desires. As Damasio describes them, emotions—"disgust, fear, happiness, sadness, sympathy, and shame—aim directly at life regulation by staving off dangers or helping the organism take advantage of an opportunity, or indirectly by facilitating social relations" (39). They are, in Brennan's terms, at the core of the "intelligence of the flesh," part of the "senses and the informational channels of the flesh that . . . are intelligent, aware, and struggling to communicate with a slower, thicker person who calls itself I" (2004, 140).

As a component of the "life drive," emotion plays out "in the theater of the body." In contrast, feelings "play out in the theatre of the mind" (Damasio 1999, 28). Feelings "translate the ongoing life state" into words and images; it is through words and images that the mind comprehends the complex and shifting reality of the body (Damasio 2003, 85). This translation from body to mind, from emotion to feeling, is mediated by the somatosensory cortex. The somatosensory cortex is the brain's internal representation of the body, a body map in which each part of the body has a corresponding neural component. Although emotions are bodily responses to the neurochemical reactions of sensory information, feelings are the perception in the brain's body map of the state of the body in relation to thought.

We shall return, in a moment, to the somatosensory cortex. For right now, though, I want to concentrate on understanding how thoughts are part of our feeling states. One way to grasp this is to think of how we experience the difference between "happiness" and "sadness." States of high happiness are associated with "rapid image change and short attention span" (Damasio 2003, 85). One pleasing thought brings to mind another, which brings to mind another; the more euphoric we are, the more pleasurable images our minds conjure, and the more quickly we jump from image to image. Sadness, on the other hand, entails "low rates of image production and hyper-attentiveness to images" (85). The sadder we are, the longer we dwell on our stockpile of bad memories. Feeling sad thus involves "an inefficient mode of thought stalling around a limited number of ideas of loss" (89).

The fact that happy states generate more happy thoughts and sad states generate more sad thoughts allows us to see that feelings have definite *themes*. They are also associated with bodily states—shallow, rapid, deep, or slow breathing; blood vessels constricting; heartbeat, pulse, or temperature changing. Feeling is thus the interaction of the "perception of a certain state of the body along with the perception of a certain mode of thinking and of thoughts with certain themes" (Damasio 2003, 86). In other words, feeling is what happens in the brain, where bodily states are registered and produce themes and modes of thinking. To shift bad feeling states, then, we have to develop language that attends to the "pathways of sensation in the body" (Brennan 2004, 153). We need to develop a language that can connect our feelings to bodily processes and emotions. And we need to learn to understand our feelings as the complicated relationship between our bodily states, our memories, and our habits of mind.

The language that brings the emotion of the body into the conscious awareness of the mind can help us interpret our feelings and understand how they work. To turn into the body, to learn to listen for what the experience of the body is trying to communicate, is to bear witness. We bear witness by giving language to what is unconscious, unwitnessed. When we do this, we can release ourselves from the grip an emotion has on us. We can maybe even transform it.

Again, psychoanalysis and neuroscience offer ways to think about what it means for our experience to be *unwitnessed* as well as what is required *to bear witness* to our experience. First, psychoanalysis. One of the foremost scholars of the Holocaust, Shoshana Felman, argues that the Holocaust transpired through a cultural failure to bear witness. Analyzing the genocide of Jews in Poland, Felman finds that victims, perpetrators, and bystanders occupied different topographical and cognitive positions.

The topographical positions—literally, where we stand, what we see from where we stand. The Polish farmer sees something different from the Polish factory worker. One will see a difference in food being ordered, used, picked up. One will see a difference in the manufacture and use of tools, textiles. They both see, from where they stand, differently from the guard at Auschwitz, at Birkenau, at Bełżec, at Chełmno, at Gross-Rosen. Each person—the Jewish child, the old woman sent immediately to her death, the soldier herding people onto trains, the Polish child whose father works in a factory—sees a different part of the same events.

The same is true for our cognitive positions—how our minds strain to see and not see, to know and not know. What will the wife see of the husband who commands a concentration camp? How will she reconcile her need to support her husband in his military career, her desire for the security of a job, a house, a paycheck, with the evidence the camp emits—weekly trainloads of prisoners, glimpses of human skeletons, the smoke from the ovens, rumors she tries not to hear. How will a worker—in a bank, a railroad station, a post office, a bakery—reconcile her suspicions about what she sees with her need for her job?

In Poland, Felman argues, people "saw" and "knew" different things based on their different topographical and cognitive positions. The Jews saw but did not "understand the purpose and destination of what they [saw]"; the Poles saw but, as bystanders, "they [did] not quite look, they avoid[ed] looking directly and thus they overlook[ed] at once their responsibility and their complicity as witness" (1992, 208); the Nazis "[saw] to it that both the Jews and the extermination [would] remain unseen, invisible" (208). The unbreachable gap between these different topographical and cognitive positions resulted in a "splitting of eyewitnessing" that, in effect, let the Holocaust occur as an event unwitnessed.

Neuroscience has a parallel to what Felman calls the "splitting of eyewitnessing." To understand the neurophysiological dimension of the splitting of eyewitnessing, we need to return to the somatosensory cortex. The brain does not simply take the raw data that it perceives through the senses and reproduce it faithfully (Kandel 2007, 302). Instead, specialized cells and nerves receive specific kinds of information and send this to equally specialized regions in the "somatosensory cortex," an area of the brain in which each part of the body is represented. It is this "map" of our bodies that receives sensory information—everything from taste, touch, smell, sound, and sights to information cueing danger or safety.

Furthermore, positron emission tomography (PET) and functional magnetic resonance imaging (fMRI) show us that neural connections "filter and transform sensory information on the way to and within the cortex," which is "organized into functional compartments or modules" (Kandel 2007, 301). More specifically, the somatosensory cortex is "organized into columns of nerve cells extending from its upper to its lower surface," and each column is dedicated to one specific area: Individual neurons in one area respond only to signals from the specific area to which they are linked. Hence, "all the cells in one column might receive information on superficial touch from the end of the index finger. Cells in another column might receive information on deep pressure from the index finger" (300).

The same is true for visual information. Cells in the retina relay information through the brain stem and the thalamus to the cortex in precise ways. And the cells of the retina do not see absolute light; they see the relation between light and dark. Some cells respond to horizontal lines of light/dark, others to vertical lines, and still others to angles. Similarly, information about motion, depths, form, and color are "segregated from one another and conveyed in separate pathways to the brain, where they are brought together and coordinated into a unified perception" (Kandel 2007, 302).

Added to all this, different parts of the body are represented in the somatosensory cortex "in proportion to [their] importance in sensory perception" (Kandel 2007, 299). The more we use or rely on a portion of our body, the larger its representation in our somatosensory cortex. Hence, a pianist has larger areas in the brain representing the fingers, a runner has larger areas representing the feet, a singer has larger areas representing the vocal chords. Different parts of the body are represented in the brain according to their importance, they receive different kinds of information, and they send sensory data along different paths to different parts of the brain.

At the level of our cells, within our own bodies and brains, we are split witnesses.

What neuroscience can still not explain is how all this "information about motion, depths, color, and form, which is carried by separate neural pathways," is integrated into an organized, cohesive perception of the world (Kandel 2007, 303). How does the brain integrate the sensory information signaled by the retina about color, depth, and motion into an image of a girl walking a dog? And how does it know the difference between any girl of twelve and your niece Jenny, walking your Pekingese poodle, Smoky?

Scientists call this unresolved mystery about how the sensory systems send electrical and chemical signals along neural pathways, how

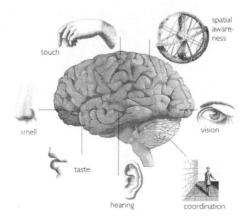

The vast majority of the cortex is given over to sensory processing—only the frontal lobes are dedicated to nonsensual tasks.

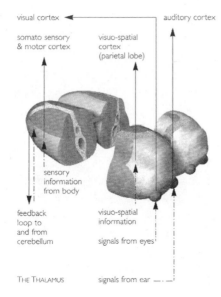

All incoming sensory information (except smell) goes first to the thalamus. This limbic nucleus acts like a relay station, shunting the data onto appropriate cortical areas for processing.

(Illustrations/captions from Rita Carter, *Mapping the Mind* [Berkeley: University of California Press, 1999], p. 115. Used with permission from University of California Press.)

the brain fires neurons and creates meaning, the "binding problem." The binding problem is the central enigma of consciousness—the question of how the brain brings all the scattered fragments of sensory data and neural firing together into integrated images and generates a coherent understanding of self and world.

Psychoanalysis and neuroscience ask us to grapple with our fragments of un-integrated information, our split positions as failed witnesses.

To grapple with our failure as witness means to ask, over and over again, how do we know what we know? What do we know that we don't know that we know?

Felman's analysis of the fragmenting of witnessing shows us that there are, in fact, witnesses who *see* and *hear* traumatic events but "*cannot understand* the significance of what is going on" (1992, 212). This is as true for our day-to-day lives as it is for the Holocaust. Myriad kinds of personal and collective violences remain unencountered, unwitnessed, even though there are people present, potential witnesses. (At five years old, I did not get out of my bed, track down the noises, name the sounds I was hearing. I did not mark on a calendar "February 2, 1969," and note the details of what was said, who was being beaten. I hid under my covers, held my breath.)

When potential witnesses overlook, fail to look, misunderstand, or hide what they see, "seeing" is unable to "translate itself spontaneously and simultaneously into a meaning" (Felman 1992, 212). This splitting of our witnessing—from our different positions, from our desires to both know and not know, from our bodies' translations of raw sensory data into words and images—can result in events that are, cognitively and conceptually, unwitnessed at both the individual and the social levels. At the individual level, as we have seen, our split positions as witness can keep us from fully "seeing" and from being able to understand what we do and do not see. At the social level, we are blind men at the elephant, each with our own un-integrated fragments. Lacking a common frame of reference, we cannot form what Felman calls a "*community of seeing*" (211).

But what does a "community of seeing" mean? In order to unfold, analyze, process, and make sense of events, we need a dialogic, relational space—we need to pool all our memory fragments to find a common language, a more complete perspective. This is the social component of the bringing into consciousness of what is unconscious in us—as individuals, as families, as communities, as societies.

A case in point: How many of us can really claim to fully take in, to really "understand," most of the situations we are in? How many miscommunications mark a normal day—when we think what we have said has been misunderstood, when we explain as clearly as we can what we mean and somebody else still turns our words another way? How many hurt feelings and eruptions of anger come upon us unaware? Moments when we could not have imagined that somebody would be hurt or angry by what we said or did, or when, without even fully knowing why, we find ourselves bursting into tears or yelling things we did not know we felt until we heard the words coming out of our mouths?

We bring the unconscious in ourselves into every communication, every social relation. Our failure to "know," then, is both individual and collective—a matter of what we do not know both within and among ourselves. To form a community of seeing is to do collectively, as a practice of our relations, the work of translation. The translation of emotion into feeling, of finding the words that let the "slower, thicker I" understand both itself and the others to whom it is in relation.

This is bulky language: "the translation of emotion into feeling, of finding the words that let the 'slower, thicker I' understand both itself and the others to whom it is in relation." But I think it is precise. If we distinguish the physical body experiencing sensations and signaling these to the brain from the processes of consciousness interpreting and making meaning of experience, then who and what is the "I"? Is it the cells of the skin "feeling"? The cells of the retina "seeing"? The cells of the nose "smelling"? The body hungry, thirsty, desiring?

And how much of the "I" is a matter of the unthought, unconscious roles we play? When we walk into a classroom, what we do and how we do it depends on whether we are playing the role of the student or the teacher. Who we "are" at any given moment depends on the different roles we have in the different places we inhabit. Try this: Pick any building, any place, any location—it doesn't matter what it is. A church. A house. A park. A jail. A hospital. A store. Now pick roles: minister/ parishioner. Host/guest. Mother/child. Baseball player/groundskeeper. Inmate/guard/warden. Nurse/doctor/patient. Cashier/customer. Now, move the nurse from the hospital to the park. Or move the prison warden from the jail to the grocery store. Now, make the doctor a woman. Or make the minister Muslim. Or make the baseball player Mexican. Does your perception of the roles and how they will be played change?

My point: Each of us follows, largely without even thinking about it, scripts for how to behave based on the social roles we are assigned and our social locations.

So we are back to the splitting of witnessing based on our different topographical and cognitive positions. Are we doing what we do in a church, on the playground, at the beach, in a classroom, at a bar, in our living room, our bedroom, the kitchen, a restaurant? Who are we in all these spaces? Without our conscious awareness, the space we are in scripts our actions. The same is true for our cognitive locations—where we "are" in our heads at any given moment. Are we angry? Sad? Happy? Afraid? We'll act differently from these different emotional places. Our beliefs also stake out cognitive positions. If we think of people as "different" from us—based on skin or sexual orientation or religion or the countries they are from—will we behave toward them the same way that we do to those we think of as the "same"?

These are important questions. They are questions that get us to the heart of what it means to form a community of seeing. Through a community of seeing, we learn to see and understand ourselves and each other, bring into consciousness what is unconscious in us as individuals and in the societies we form.

Without a community of seeing, we continue our suffering. We stay in the grip of our emotions—our fear, our anger, our shame, our pain. We fail to comprehend the meaning of events, of our actions. Without a community of seeing, we are locked into violences we cannot escape. Whatever violence it is—Dachau or Darfur or the rapes that take place every four minutes in America or the beatings that happen in our homes or the women whose clitorises are cut off or the gays and lesbians who are killed—all our violences, small or large, take place through the splitting of our topographical and cognitive positions, through the inability to fully comprehend the meaning of events and actions, through the failure to bear witness. The Polish worker who fails to give a name to the smoke coming from the chimneys at Auschwitz. The child who hides under the covers and fails to locate or define the sounds of violence that wake her up.

All our violences rely on the same process of splitting and fragmentation, the same failures to comprehend and hence bear witness. This is not to say that all violences are the same. They are not. But it is to say that they are on a continuum. The violences of Dachau and Darfur rely on the small, unremarkable violences of our day-to-day lives.

6

IF I SHOULD DIE
BEFORE I WAKE

When the haunted house busted our ghosts out, Georgia became my lifeline: the one I could call when I awoke at three in the morning with dreams of Frank trying to kill me, the one who had concrete memories, the one who let me know I was not crazy. For years and years, I dreamed constantly, always the same thing: that somebody was trying to kill me, to shoot me because I had told. In the dreams, what I had "told" was never clear. But, morning after morning, I awoke terrified that I would be shot. I awoke in the middle of the night with my head being drilled, my stomach sawed open. I awoke trapped in a car with Frank on an army base. Some nights, I was so frozen with terror that I locked myself in my room with my German shepherd, my Doberman pinscher, my .22 rifle, and my shotgun—my "protection."

I could go months with reoccurring nightmares, three and four days in a row without sleep. Sometimes, I thought my nightmares were going to kill me. I'd wake with my heart pounding so hard that I thought I was having a heart attack; wake too dizzy to stand, with my vision blurred and my head so split by pain that I was sure I was having a stroke. My dreams turned my body against itself, leaving my nerves pulsing, my skin crawling, my insides turned out. I tried everything to shut my body up and get back to sleep. I exercised, I watched TV, I ate, I got drunk. Food was best at stretching my skin tight and blocking out the images of chasing, shooting, killing. I could eat until I was nauseated, until nausea took over my body and wouldn't let anything else in. I could eat until I threw up, threw out the chaos in my body and my insides could finally rest. Trying to stop my body's screaming, trying to shake this fog and confusion, trying to get sleep, I gained sixty pounds.

My dreaming exhausted me, drained all my energy and imagination away. In those days, I seldom wrote my dreams down. I just wanted to forget them. But some of them I couldn't shake.

> *I am having such violent dreams. They affect me throughout the day, it is hard to get up and to get any energy to work. Exhausted! Depressed. Last night, I dreamed that the land was bombed, smoking chaos and guerrilla fighters, assassins on the remaining buildings. A paramilitary group set up encampment in the yard of my house, and on my porch a fighter was beginning to rape a woman he had captured. I cried, screamed, begged a nearby military man to make him stop, to NOT let him do this.*

Throughout all these years, Georgia listened to my dreaming.

One day, talking to Kathrin about my nightmares, I wondered if I needed to learn how to be my own father. In the first years of our work together, Kathrin had taught me how to comfort and nurture myself, how to be my own mother. But these months-long marathon nightmares required something different, something I had not learned yet.

Kathrin asked me, "What would a good father do?"

I didn't know. All I could say was that he would "protect" me. He wouldn't let anything "bad" happen to his children.

Kathrin said a good father does more than "protect" his children. He stimulates them in the right way—teaches them how to engage in the world, take risks, learn their own strength. A "good" father would show me how to discover my own power.

And she asked me this: If Kashif—my protector friend, my partner, who was showing me the best part of what "men" could be—were in my dreams, what would he do?

That was easy. If Kashif were in my dream, he would fight back, not flee. He would not stop to bandage wounds and count the dead until he had killed the enemy.

Sitting in Kathrin's office, exhausted after interminable months of nightmares and insomnia, I felt like I was the walking wounded in this world of pain. Kathrin told me to fly my wounds like a flag, to wear them like a medal. She said that I may be battle scarred, but the scar could be my mark of life, not my insignia of death.

A mark of life? Flag? Medal? What could that possibly mean?

I left Kathrin's office and went to the gym, where I had spent four years weight training and making myself strong. On the exercise bike, trying to understand what Kathrin's words could mean, I remembered a time when I was fourteen and Frank punched me. It was a day that I had been happy. I'd taken my Pekingese poodle, Smoky, for a walk through the orange groves, past the locks, along the canal off Lake Tohopekaliga. Feeling the force of my own life energy, simultaneously light and strong, I walked miles and miles into a horizon of water and sky. In my own mind, I was my beloved Bilbo Baggins, chasing dragons, ready to walk until I found God, until I understood the meaning of life. When I returned to the campground, Frank was lying in wait for me. He was in a jealous rage. He accused me of being with men. I tried to explain the meaning-of-life feeling, but he couldn't hear a word I said. He screamed:

"Liar!"

"Slut!"

Balled up fist coming at my face. Stunned disbelief. My skin trying to crawl under my bones and away from the impact.

On an exercise bike in the Gainesville Women's Health and Fitness Center, I remembered all this like it was happening to me again, remembered it in a way that made me forget where I was. I slipped between times. I relived this scene, right down to the moment when Frank punched me and I ran, crying, into the cow pasture bordering the park. But, in my re-membering, instead of crying and running, I turned around and began to beat Frank. I screamed at him, called him a bastard, a bully, a tyrant. I fought back.

In a moment of expiation, I understood what Kathrin meant when she said to imagine what Kashif would do if he were confronted with an enemy—he would fight. He would not run and repair the wounds, tend the sick, pick up the pieces; he would enter the fray and fight the enemy. Seventeen years after that punching, I could finally turn around and fight back.

That exercise bike was not the first place I had fought the effects of Frank in my life. I fought the effects of him when I began to think something was wrong with him running off with his niece and stranding Mother in a campground. I fought the effects of him when I got a good therapist, when I broke the injunction to silence that he had imposed on all of us. I fought the effects of him when I went to my sisters and said, "Help me remember," and when I refused my ex-husband's verbal and sometimes physical violence. I fought the effects of him when I realized that his jealous rages were not my fault. So, falling through a hole in time on that exercise bike was not the first time I stood up and fought the effects of Frank in my life. But it was the first time I realized that Frank was, after all, just a man: an old man, pushing seventy, and that, if I really wanted to, I could turn around and beat the shit out of him.

After that, my nightmares became places where I could continue fighting the effects of Frank, one dimension of the work of rescripting my inheritance. Like in the fall of 1995, when, for almost three months, I dreamed the same thing: I had checked out some computer disks that I needed for my research from the army, but, before returning them, I made copies. The military was trying to get these disks back and to kill me. Night after night, I would wake up just before I was caught and shot, terrified. During the long months of this dreaming, I enlisted the help of my witnesses. Kathrin had taught me to talk to my dreams. Ask them questions. Think of them like a story. What is this story telling, and, if I could enter this story and change anything, what would it be? This wasn't exactly easy—the killing, the blood, the fear of dying were real, present, inside me. But Kathrin said: Is something trying to be born out of the dying? Could I imagine that all the characters could be some part of me? So, if somebody is drilling a hole through my head, is something inside my head that the driller is trying to get? What part of me could that be?

I learned how to look at the scene of my dreaming. Where was I? Who and what else was present in my dream world? If I turned the people in my dreams into characters in a story I was writing, what would I have each of them do differently? If my dream were a story, with a plot that was still open, evolving, how would I write the next scene? My friend Virginia was especially good at talking through my dreams with me. She entered the plot like an adventurer, an explorer, full of curiosity. Creatively. She brought psychoanalytic theory to our conversations but never an "interpretation." She asked questions, wondered out loud, held onto the threads we were untangling.

A little over a month into the questions I was asking of my army-trying-to-kill-me dream, one of my professors appeared: John, a critical theorist, who would be able to decipher the information on my computer disks. And who, like my grandmother Lily, spoke French. I gave him my identity papers—my passport, my driver's license, my car keys, my copy of the computer disks. Shortly after this, the dream changed. I was no longer simply running from the army that was trying to kill me. I was, instead, trying to capture the people who were chasing me. Finally, the last night I had this dream, I was holding a séance, trying to conjure the people chasing me. My father appeared, at the head of the army. In this room, with all my witnesses in a circle conjuring the dead, my father and the army were powerless. I have not had this dream since.

So what do these dreams "mean?" And how much does "knowing" what all the dream symbols mean really matter, anyway? At the time that I was having the army dream, I talked with all my witnesses about the characters, the scenes, the army trying to kill me. After almost two months of this talking, two elements in an otherwise repetitive nightmare sequence changed: John appeared, and, instead of simply running from the army, I began trying to capture the people trying to kill me. It was easy enough, at the time, to see that John was a part of myself I needed to access—smart, accomplished, somebody who would know how to interpret information that, uninterpreted, put me at risk. Once I transferred my "identity" to him—the passport, driver's license, student I.D. card—I began to fight back. But it was years later before I realized that John carried another meaning. He speaks French, like my grandmother Lily, the first person to stand up to Frank. And he appeared in the dream wearing a Hawaiian shirt and lei, symbols from the place I was first able to tell my father that I would not keep his secrets anymore. Looking back over a distance of several years, I can say that one of the reasons this nightmare was able to shift is that John's appearance symbolically made available the option of fighting back. But at the time I was having this nightmare, I could not have made this interpretation, could not have said all the things that John's character "meant."

Similarly, the night my father finally appeared in the dream, it ended. At the time, I could say that the séance was a place where my witnesses and I were calling on the dead to find out who was trying to kill me and so to be able to capture them. And I could say that, when my father appeared at the head of the army, I had found out what I needed to know—all along, "the army" and "Frank" had meant the same thing, and, once I identified Frank, the dream was done. In retrospect, I think that séance scene "means" something more than I thought it meant when I was having the dream. I think now that I was calling all the ghosts of all the pasts that have been living, unmet and unresolved, in my family. But, again, I did not need to "know" that to do the dream work that freed me from this nightmare. My point: Our "meanings" shift, grow, evolve over time. Any naming—to say this means such and such or that means so and so—is a transitory thing. We name precisely so as to be able to mark a point and move on. It is the *direction* in which our naming lets us *move* that matters. To forget this is to fixate on the small point—whatever naming we have so far been able to achieve, whatever meaning we have so far been able to make—and fail to see the more important *process*.

Within the fields of science and psychology, a great deal of controversy still exists about what dreams "mean." At one extreme end of the spectrum, some neuroscientists see dreams as neural noise, the by-product of the sleeping brain doing its equivalent of housekeeping. From this perspective, the sleeping brain is busy strengthening important neural connections, forming new connections that encode experience from the day into long-term memory, and throwing out irrelevant, redundant, and unnecessary data. At the other extreme, psychoanalysts see dreams as important symbolic representations of internal states—unconscious conflicts, desires, emotions. From this perspective, the content of dreams, far from being meaningless, is important material that we can analyze and decode and from which we can learn and grow.

The neural noise explanation of dreams does not offer much help either to people experiencing chronic and debilitating nightmares or to the practitioners working with them. Most practitioners working in this culture recognize that chronic nightmares can be an important symptom of the traumas for which they are treating their patients, but, even so, a great deal of disagreement exists about what the nightmares "mean" and how to work with them. Until recently, the bulk of work on nightmares in patients with posttraumatic stress disorders had come out of research on war veterans, and this research focused on the ways that nightmares repeat the traumatic events of war. In these patients, nightmares tend to represent the literal repetition of events that soldiers experienced; they redream the scene of violence, often with vivid sensory details about what they saw, smelled, heard, tasted, touched.

This research provides little help for understanding or working with the kinds of nightmares that return us to scenes of our childhood, though. Nor does it help us understand how the chronic, structuring, pervasive violence that so many children grow up in can return as nightmares in adult life. What if the violence a child lives occurs, literally, in the dark? What images does a mind find to represent the source of threat? And what if violence occurs in another room? How does the mind find forms to represent the terror of what is heard? And what if a child is very young—age one, or two, or three? And does not have the language with which to understand what she hears, what she sees? If violence is unsignifiable—if it has sounds, and smells, and touch, but neither words nor images that can represent it—how does a nightmare repeat an "event"?

But understanding what "nightmare" means under such circumstances is even more complicated than this. At five years old, we understand the world differently from the way we did when we were two. And at ten, we understand differently from when we were five. And so on. How much we can understand a thing and find words to give it meaning depends on our cognitive and linguistic capacities. Our language and our mental powers grow as we grow so that we gain more and more language to describe a world that we can see in more complexity at fifteen, twenty, twenty-five years old. At each stage of our cognitive and linguistic growth, we develop more nuanced understandings of people, events, relationships, ourselves. The world takes on new meanings. Some meanings we give up: Santa Claus, the Easter Bunny, the Tooth Fairy. Some meanings we adjust: what makes a movie "good" or what counts as "fun" on a weekend. Other things, though, "signify" but defy "meaning." The difference between the clingy-lacy-sexy pajamas your father buys you and the cotton nightclothes your friends wear. Seeing your sister living under a bridge while your father wears black and says she is dead. How much of what we dream is part of the work of reseeing such pasts as these? Of developing new ways of understanding them, of forging new meanings?

For years and years, my nightmares chased my sleep away. Although neuroscientists disagree about why the brain needs sleep to perform some of its vital functions, they do agree that sleep is important to both learning and survival. Learning to survive my nightmares was thus, at a fundamental level, a life-and-death affair. First, I learned how to live through the days of am-I-having-a-heart-attack-stroke-no-no-no-don't-sleep-can't-sleep-I-will-die-he-will-kill-me dreams. Gradually, Kathrin taught me how to use my nightmares to restage the scene of danger—I could be the one who wins.

Like in this dream: A man had raped a child and was going to get away with it. In this dream, there were many witnesses. Some were bystanders, helplessly watching, able to do nothing. Some were accomplices, either actively assisting the rapist or passively allowing him to continue his actions. Some, however, were my helpers. My first witness, Denise, was in this dream, as were my mother and sisters. At the end of an exceedingly long, complicated nightmare, I had chased the rapist into a park, where two other women and I beat him flat, into text:

I am very conscious that I have to be very careful, to swing only when I know I can hit him. Then I beat him. Beat him, beat him, beat him. I feel his body go limp. He is cut and bruised and torn, and I am beating him, beating him, beating him. All the while, I am afraid that somebody might have gotten the gun from Denise, from whom he must have escaped, so I am worried about somebody finding me and shooting me. I successfully beat him, and then another woman that he had raped comes, and she wants to beat him too. She picks up a hammer and begins beat-

ing him. A third woman comes and also beats him with a hammer, and we are beating him flat, into text.

Then somebody has the idea to pulverize his wrist, which we begin doing. This is a very delicate operation . . . we have to hold his arm just right, and I have the slight fear that he might come to and grab us with the hand that we have to get hold of to position the wrist for pulverizing. The three of us do this successfully. At this point, his arm breaks off, and I realize he is dead. So we have to decide what to do with him, and because we have beaten him flat to paper, we tear him.

I have lived so many years of my life with nightmares, and so many more with dreaming that seems to be freeing something up in me, that I do not buy a strictly "neural noise" theory of dreaming. Clearly, there is an important work that my dreams are doing and an important work that I do with and through them. But I also do not think everything I dream "means" something, and, even in the dreams that clearly carry symbolic meaning, I could not always say what that meaning might be. What I do know: Once I started recording my dreams and bringing my daytime and my nighttime worlds into relation, the dreams started to change. I turned my nightmares into stories, texts that I was writing. I enlisted my witnesses in the daytime world in the project of rescripting my dreaming. I started sleeping with my laptop. It was my guarantee of sleep, my amulet against the terror of my dreams. No matter what violence woke me up in the middle of the night, I could immediately write it out, turn it into a story, something with which I could work. I became an explorer of my fear, charting its effects on my body, the signs and symbols it left in my psyche.

This was not easy work to take up. At times, I thought I might die from the terror of my dreams:

Dreaming again. This time, my father is trying to kill me. I have escaped from the car and am running down the road, but people appear who not only will not help me but seem to be on his side. A woman who had been trying to help me gives up when a truck full of men helping my father appears. She says, "She's all yours, boys," and so I think I am lost now, have no help.

When I wake up, I think I am going to die of a heart attack. I call Kathrin and ask her, "Can people die of a heart attack when they are dreaming?" I tell her about my father chasing me and my heart feeling like it is going to explode and not being able to breathe, about the blackness in my head, the dizziness, how I cannot stand and the throwing up and I cannot stop crying. She talks to me until I can breathe and my heart stops pounding blood into my temples and tells me how I can sip water to help bring my crying under control.

Despite all the times I thought I might die—and the few times that, in my nighttime world, I did—my nightmares did not kill me. At least, not literally. Symbolically, though, those nighttime battles laid to rest some old ghosts. In very crucial ways, I have come to think of my nightmares as performing the work of mourning. Mourning requires that we let some meanings die—old identities, old ways of seeing ourselves, our relations—in order to forge new possibilities for our living. If we have been shaped by distorted notions of "love," "marriage," "family," then the ways that we look for love, enter into marriage, participate in family will be distorted too. We cannot find healthier, more productive ways of loving and living as long as we are being twisted and contorted by the distorted ideas we inherited. I think of my nightmares as the place where my psyche fought the battles that liberated new possibilities for being in the world. Liberating new possibilities, however, requires letting go of old patterns, old identities. To "let go" of an identity is not easy—it is a threat, a loss, a breaking-open of an old self, a free fall into the not-yet-born identities we are making. It is equivalent to a dying, and it requires our mourning.

Some of my dreams make this work of mourning explicit. Once, in the early days of working on this book, I dreamed that I had returned to the house where Frank, Mother, and Georgia still lived. The house was a place of sickness and fear, playing out, still, the family relations of my childhood.

There was great fear in the house—big fear. I knew this, and I was—not angry, because my sadness was so big and such a

weight, that nothing else could rise above that weight—but I was
HARD somehow, like a rock. But not a rock to be thrown. I was a
rock that would hold things down, in place.

Somebody told me to be careful about where I slept, to which
I said, "I will sleep where I want to!" I refused to be afraid, was
determined that Frank would just have to sleep in his room. He
could not move this rock that I was. Georgia came in, and then
Mother. They were ashamed, hurt. I started to say, "Why the
fuck do you do that?" to my mother but stopped my words as
the rock and the sadness in me felt that it didn't really matter.
Mother started to cry, and then my rock and my sadness moved
to her, and I just held her, with her head on my shoulder, and
stroked her hair, and told her, "Don't worry. Everything will be
all right."

In very real ways, to write this book has been a process of returning to that house to continue the work of letting go of old meanings, old ways of being. The dreaming, the writing, the mourning are all part of the same work of liberating new possibilities for a future that I have to imagine differently. As grief work, then, these nightmares are not so much the literal signs of what happened in the past as they are treasure maps pointing the way to my future. My nightmares, like the future, are still open: My past is there, rupturing its way into the present, but the rupture offers a possibility for moving differently into a future that I am in the process of making.

Kathrin showed me how to enter this process. She insisted on rewards: At the end of every nightmare, every panic attack, I had to celebrate my survival, to congratulate myself for the courage it took to let my body spill its insides out. And she resisted simple, easy explanations. She wanted me to play with multiple meanings, to learn to live with ambiguity, to be creative. It is my fear, she said, that makes me want to construct a simple cause-effect story, to say, "Frank is this and that," and "I suffer because of what Frank did." We want to beat down contradictions, to make stories that keep "good" and "bad" separate. Our lives are not, however, a matter or either/or; we are, rather, always circling around the both/and. It takes courage to let our contradictions exist, to accept our multiple meanings, to endure the flood of emotion that overwhelms and engulfs us when traumatic pasts force their presence upon us. But our histories are always there, trailing us. If we cannot bring our past to the surface, look at and understand it, we do not possess it—it possesses us.

INTERLUDE III

On Bearing Witness
to the Process of Witnessing

D ori Laub, a psychoanalyst who has spent his career working with survivors of the Holocaust, argues that our inability to find the language to speak about the histories possessing us leaves us helpless subjects in the hands of the tyrant past. Past events "become more and more distorted in their silent retention and pervasively invade and contaminate the survivor's daily life. The longer the story remains untold, the more distorted it becomes in the survivor's conception of it" (1992, 79). To tell the stories of our pasts allows us to repossess our histories, to reclaim ownership of our own life stories.

As we have already seen, the pasts that possess us have remained unwitnessed and hence incomprehensible to us. We may be able to describe the symptoms of our unwitnessed pasts—the destructive actions we repeat over and over again, the fears, angers, depressions against which we are helpless—without ever *understanding* them. The long, slow, painstaking labor of repossessing ourselves by bearing witness to the pasts that possess us is a process. It is a process that requires the right conditions and the right kind of witness.

Elizabeth Jelin, writing about the problems of working through histories of state repression—torture, disappearances, civil war, the too many brutalities that have become the background of our lives—argues that working through traumatic symptoms requires social spaces for memory circulation. In social conditions that enforce silence, "victims can find themselves isolated and trapped in a ritualized repetition of their pain, without any access to the possibility of dialogue and to a friendly environment for working through their suffering" (2003, 44–45). Repossessing ourselves requires an "empathic listener," an *addressable other* "who can hear the anguish of one's memories and thus affirm and recognize their realness" (Jelin 2003, 65; Laub 1992, 68). The addressable other is one who can hear the story, who can recognize and respond to the speaker. But to hear—to *recognize* and *respond*—is not an easy matter. It requires, as Jelin argues, "'others' with the ability to ask, to express curiosity for a painful past, as well as to have compassion and empathy" (2003, 65). And it requires the even more difficult commitment to remain present and steady in the face of the rupture through which the unwitnessed history emerges.

I have come to think of this process of witnessing as holding the space of the rupture. It requires holding open the door between the here and now and the there and then. In the there and then, there is pain, grief, and terror. To hold that door open is to allow the pain, grief, and terror into the present. The witness keeps the one who has to walk up to that door and look through it from falling into the there and then and from being lost to the past that is emerging. Laub describes the witness as the one who can provide an independent frame of reference through which the past can be observed in the present (1992, 81). In the past, no witnesses could really see, really understand, or really give meaning to events. Through the witness, the survivor returns to the past so as to enunciate experience and hence incorporate it into "life in the present and the future" (Jelin 2003, 72). Fundamentally, the process of witnessing is a process of re-membering *for* a future. The pasts that remain unwitnessed condemn us to cycles of endless repetition; to find the language to bring the past into the present allows us to loosen the oppressive hold that the past has on us.

Laub explains this process of bearing witness as the process of coming to know our life stories "unimpeded by ghosts from the past" against which we have had to protect ourselves. The process of witnessing is the process by which we come to know our buried truths in order to imagine futures with meaning and hope (1992, 78). The process requires both a return *to* and a return *from* the pasts that must be witnessed. To hold the space of the rupture, the witness must be able to withstand the force of the pain that enters the present, to keep the door between past and present open through the return *to* and *from* the past that must be brought into language. The witness needs to be able to walk right up to the lip of the abyss, to remain a steady presence while the one looking struggles for the language to name what she is seeing. As much as anything else, it is this *struggle* that is being witnessed. The struggle involves retreats, waiting, processing, backing up, and moving forward again. It is a haltering, faltering alternation between "moving closer and then retreating from the experience" (76).

To bear witness is thus to participate in the journey to and return from the lip of the abyss. "What ultimately matters in all processes of witnessing . . . is not simply the information, the establishment of the facts, but the experience itself of *living through* testimony, of giving testimony" (Laub 1992, 85). The process of finding the language to bring the past into the present is the process of seeing for ourselves what we have left unwitnessed, of becoming witness to our own pasts and thus repossessing them (rather than being possessed by them). It is the process through which we reclaim our own life stories.

My witnesses—Kathrin, Joyce, Kashif, Virginia, Denise, Georgia, all the people who went through my nightmares with me—brought me to lip of the abyss and held me steady while I repossessed my past. This is one of the gifts that has allowed me to live.

7

THE PASTS WE REPEAT I

Margaret

In Plum Village in France, we receive many letters from the refugee camps in Singapore, Malaysia, Indonesia, Thailand, and the Philippines, hundreds each week. . . . One day we received a letter telling us about a young girl on a small boat who was raped by a Thai pirate. She was only twelve, and she jumped into the ocean and drowned herself. When you first learn of something like that, you get angry at the pirate. You naturally take the side of the girl. As you look more deeply you will see it differently. If you take the side of the little girl, then it is easy. You only have to take a gun and shoot the pirate. But we cannot do that. In my meditation, I saw that if I had been born in the village of the pirate and raised in the same conditions as he was, I am now the pirate. There is a great likelihood that I would become a pirate. . . . If you or I were born today in those fishing villages, we might become sea pirates in twenty-five years. If you take a gun and shoot the pirate, you shoot all of us, because all of us are to some extent responsible for this state of affairs.

THICH NHAT HANH, *BEING PEACE*

When Frank got back from Vietnam, he was obsessed with getting away from "civilization" and "back to the land." He requested a transfer to Fort Greely, Alaska, where he could live out his dream of hunting and fishing in an uncontaminated wilderness. For over two years, we left the lower forty-eight behind; we moved to an isolated subarctic army base with no family history, nothing to hold or sustain memories. No witnesses.

Alaska was Frank's last duty station. When he retired from the army, he moved us to Satsuma, Florida, a small town where Lily and Margaret were living. When we left Alaska, I didn't know anything about the history that Margaret was carrying or why Lily and Frank hated each other. I didn't know that, within six months of coming back—not to a home or to a place where we belonged, but to the witnesses Frank had left behind—Margaret's life would be torn apart for the second time.

Margaret

Margaret, for me, begins in Satsuma, Florida, the year Frank retired from the army and drove us from Alaska's winter to Lily's trailer. This was the year of the 140-degree temperature swing; in the middle of my second grade year, Frank traded in 70 degrees below 0 and Mount McKinley for 70 above and the mother-in-law he hated. I "met" Margaret in a cramped trailer spilling out people, in a place that was hot in January and had moss growing on trees and where the water smelled like rotten eggs. This was a strange and alien place, and the people I was meeting—my sister, my nieces and nephew, my grandmother—were as strange and alien as the weather and the moss and the water.

What I remember from those months in Satsuma is sweltering heat, vying for floor space in front of the fan, desperately trying to cool off. Seven of us sleeping wherever we could find a cool surface or a current of air—the living room floor, outside on a cot under the awning. What with the rotten-egg water and the moss and the problem of finding airflow, "Margaret" barely registered to me. She had children—Simon, Sandra, Marnie, and Jenny—my nephew and nieces. Simon was in middle school—in my mind, that made him "big" and hence very little to do with me. Sandra was six months older than me, Marnie six months younger, and Jenny was an infant. She had had operations for her club feet and wore braces on her legs.

We stayed with Lily until Frank could buy his own trailer, which he set up next to hers. We lived in Satsuma less than a year, just long enough for Frank to "establish" himself in the civilian world. He got a job at a paper mill, where he worked until he found a job as a park ranger at Bahia Honda State Park in the Florida Keys. We were hardly in Satsuma any time at all—just long enough for the old history of children severed from their parents to repeat itself. Long enough for the ghosts of Frank's parents, Ervin and Velma, to inhabit us. Long enough for the unresolved history of Massachusetts to catch us up in it.

———————

Like Mother, Margaret is tight-lipped about her past. She says, "The past cannot be changed, it does no good to dwell on it."

I think: She has pain she does not want to revisit, shame, anger, helplessness, years of imposed silence.

But this is me speaking about Margaret, a woman who has had so many words put in her mouth, so much of what she says ignored. Margaret would say, "It's over now; why go back there?"

How can I answer that? Except to say that the only way for me to find a self and a life and a future has been to retrace a past that, by the time I started looking for it, had already become a ghost town.

After the car wreck that killed her father, Margaret was left with one leg shorter than the other and a spinal curvature. Like Bernie, Zane, and Mother, she has bones, hips, joints that remember metal folding in on itself, bodies crushed together.

Mother is alive today because of Margaret—a nine-year-old who looked at the car wrapped around her mother, steering wheel kissing collar bone, windshield a shawl, metal and flesh weaving in and out, and said, "My mother is alive. You have to get her out of the car."

When Margaret told me about this night, she said, "They thought Mother was dead, and they wanted me to get in the ambulance."

"How did you get them to listen to you?"

"I just wouldn't get in the ambulance."

"How did you know Mother was alive?"

"I just knew," she said.

Mother never fully recovered from the wreck that killed her first husband. As it is, she has spent most of the rest of her life living out the consequences of this wreck: years in wheelchairs and on crutches, surgeries as a way of life, crippling arthritis. This has meant different things for all of us. For Margaret, this meant taking on more of a mother's duties: cooking, cleaning, looking after younger children. And, when Frank came, other things—things polite people do not talk about.

Mother was pregnant when Frank was being investigated for molesting Margaret. After the investigation, Frank abandoned his failed attempt to find the American Dream in the mill town of his childhood; he turned back to the army and the identity of soldier. With his new family in tow—a wife, three stepdaughters, and a newborn son—he signed his reenlistment papers, picked up his rifle, put on his camouflage fatigues, and left Massachusetts for good.

Between her childhood in Massachusetts and my meeting her in Satsuma, Margaret had gotten married, had three children, gotten divorced, remarried, and gotten divorced again. She was with her third husband, her fourth child an infant, when we moved from Alaska to Florida, with the unwitnessed past packed in our bags and ready to explode us all open. And, through all that, Lily had been with her. She was there when Margaret's first marriage collapsed. She put Margaret through cosmetology school. She took her in between husbands. And they were together in Satsuma when we moved back into the middle of an argument that had been raging for almost twenty years.

According to Mother: Lily's friend Mrs. Baker was going to report Margaret to the Department of Child Welfare for neglecting her children. Her husband used drugs, and the house they were living in was dilapidated, falling apart. It was Lily and her friend who thought Margaret was an unfit mother, who wanted to take the children from her. In Mother's mind, Frank was trying to help Margaret. He wanted to stop Lily from getting custody of the children, so he convinced Margaret to send the three older children back to their father in St. Louis. It was supposed to be temporary, just until Margaret could get her life straightened out. Margaret kept her infant, Jenny, with her, and was going to get Simon, Sandra, and Marnie back from their father when she got herself settled.

The silence where Margaret's voice should be: Margaret's guilt and shame are such heavy weights that it is difficult to talk to her about Satsuma, about her children being taken away from her. In the few conversations we have had about the kids going back to their father, all she can say is, "They thought I was a bad mother."

Margaret believed, when she and Frank put Simon, Sandra, and Marnie on that plane, that they were coming back. She wrote to them. When they didn't write back, she believed they were happy with their father, that they thought—like Frank, like Lily—that she was a bad mother, did not deserve to have them, was not good enough for them. She wrote until her shame stopped her, until the belief that her children did not want her dried her ink, shriveled her paper.

Years later, when we were adults and back in touch, I told Sandra that Margaret had written to them. Sandra said they never got the letters.

In 1954, Margaret was caught between Frank, who said, "This is what boys will want to do to you," and Lily, who said, "Don't let anybody fiddle with you." In 1972, she was still trapped, still feeling like things were falling apart and it was all her fault. Helpless. Shamed. Guilty. Blamed.

Shortly after Simon, Sandra, and Marnie left, so did we. Frank took a job at Bahia Honda, in the Florida Keys. Margaret moved to California with her husband and Jenny. Lily moved back to New Orleans. For the next several years, we were all in a constant state of motion.

Three years after she had to send her children to their father, Simon wrecked a dune buggy and had to have his leg amputated. Margaret flew to St. Louis to see him, where she found Simon, sixteen, one leg and one stump, angry, already lost to her and well on the road to losing himself. When Simon, Sandra, and Marnie went back to live with their father, he had a new wife and an infant daughter. Young, new to marriage and motherhood, she did not want the ex-wife's children. She beat them. Once, she beat Simon so badly that he had to be taken to the hospital. He escaped through combinations of alcohol and street drugs and racing dune buggies. Which is how he lost his leg.

Margaret sat with her son through his hospitalization, then returned to Florida without him. I can only imagine how the hours with her lost son tore her heart apart, ripped her insides out. How memories of the wreck that killed her father must have flooded back to her; months in the hospital, bodies that would never heal, lives changed forever. As a child, she stood in the face of her father's death and insisted that her mother be cut out of the car, her life saved. Then, Frank came. I can only wonder how she struggled with the knowledge that her children were being beaten and her memories of her two fathers: Patrick, who "drank and hit Mother," and Frank, who "just drank and sometimes touched her."

Three years after her children had been taken away from her, she still had no home to take them to, no way to support them. As a child, she demanded that firefighters cut her mother out of the car after the wreck that killed her father. As a mother, she could do nothing to save her son—not his leg or his spirit or, in the end, his life.

INTERLUDE IV

The Uncanny Return

This is the uncanny return. We are all familiar with the traumatic repetitions of old, destructive patterns. Choosing an alcoholic spouse when our parents were alcoholics. Staying in physically abusive relationships when we come from homes marked by domestic violence. But some repetitions of traumas seem to be almost random, do not show on the surface the signs of repeating old patterns. Dori Laub notes this particularly in the Holocaust survivors with whom he has worked. Martin Gray, for example, lost his entire family "in the flames of Warsaw and Treblinka" (1992, 65). Years later, after remarrying, establishing a home and family, he lost, for the second time, his family, his home, his possessions, all that constituted his world, to a forest fire. He writes:

> At that time, too, I could save nothing but my naked life. I escaped from fields of ruins, I fled from sewers and from Treblinka, and not one of those that had been mine remained alive. . . .
>
> Later, it seemed that after all my loneliness, the time had come for me to find my peace: my wife, the children. But then that blaze, Tanneron in flames, the crackling of the fire, that smell, that heat—just like Warsaw. Once again everything was

taken away from me, everything that seemed to have been given to me as a present: a wife, children, a life. For the second time I remained alone, with nothing but my life. (Gray, quoted in Laub 1992, 66)

Laub finds this kind of traumatic repetition consistently appearing in the lives of his patients, events that occur as though by coincidence, that could never be predicted, and that uncannily restage an earlier trauma. No matter how hard we try to repress and forget the traumatic ruptures of our lives, those things that we try to repress, that we shy "away from *knowing* and *grieving*," will resurface through life events. They come back as "haunting memory," both "through the actual return of the trauma and through its inadvertent repetition, or transmission, from one generation to another" (1992, 67).

Frank's childhood, written into Margaret, repeated with Simon, Sandra, and Marnie.

What is so interesting to me about the uncanny return is how much the traumatic repetition seems to rely on chance, on a random and unpredictable string of events. That Gray's house and second family burned and so recreated for him the experience of Warsaw. That we would leave Alaska for Florida and use Margaret and Lily as the perfect stage upon which Frank could repeat the unresolved trauma of his own childhood. His mother was called "unfit," unable to properly care for her children. He and his brother, Thomas, were sent to live with his older sister Ida. Frank restaged all this, re-creating Margaret as his mother, trapping Simon, Sandra, and Marnie up in his failed script of children sent away.

I cannot know what Lily was restaging, either in Massachusetts or in Florida. But I am sure that Lily and Frank were locked in a power struggle into which each of them carried ghosts of unresolved pasts repeating themselves. Across generations. Uncannily, turning children, grandchildren, into mirrors reflecting back pasts that have remained unwitnessed.

8

THE PASTS WE REPEAT II

Jenny

Simon, Sandra, and Marnie did not see Margaret again until 1992, and, when they did, it was at Jenny's memorial service.

Jenny's life and death still haunt me. When I left for New York in the summer of '82—the summer of Frank and Sally—Jenny was ten years old, living in a campground not far from us. Lily was in the Good Samaritan nursing home, where Margaret worked as a floor nurse. I loved Jenny. Fiercely. Devotedly. In the abstract. I was never out of crisis long enough to give Jenny concrete love. The summer I was fleeing with a man I had just met, Jenny clung to me and cried. She begged me to take her with me. She said I was leaving her behind, and asked how I could do that. But I did—I left, trying to find a way to save myself, and all she got from me was my old Schwinn ten-speed.

I wanted to take her to New York with me, wanted to write to her and have her visit, wanted her to come on summer vacations, at Christmas. But I had my own series of crises to navigate. I was nineteen, living with a man I'd known for two months—how could I take care of Jenny? Our family script kept repeating itself: Mother, nineteen, married to man she had known less than a year, giving birth to Margaret while her husband was at war. Margaret, nineteen years old when Simon was born. Children ourselves, looking for a life that could save us.

Jenny was never an easy child, never let us complacently pretend that everything was "all right." She dropped out of school, lived with one bad-for-her man after another, always needed money and help getting out of trouble. Jenny lived fucked-up outright. (I lived fucked-up in secret, hiding insomnia and nightmares and bulimia and a husband that sometimes hit me behind good grades and college degrees and my frenzied desire for a "better" life.) But no matter what Jenny did, Margaret always bailed her out, took her in, took her back, took care of her. Like Lily with her. Like Lily with Mother.

One night, Jenny called me in the middle of a physical fight she was having with one of her boyfriends. I asked her, "Why do you keep repeating the same cycles of abuse over and over again?"

Jenny said, "It's better to be fucked and then hit than not fucked at all, because the only way I know if I am loved is if I am fucked."

Jenny got fucked all right—by Frank, by older boys in New Orleans, by the series of men she hooked up with in her desperate attempts to find "love." And by me, who left a ten-year-old with an old bicycle but no address and no phone number.

I want to defend myself against my self-accusations: I want to say, "I didn't know the address yet, of the little second-story apartment I was moving to. I didn't yet have a phone."

Frank, I think, would defend himself like this. For everything I remember, wouldn't he have a similar excuse?

In the end, what good are our defenses?

In October 1991, Jenny had surgery for brain cancer. Three globular tumors, collectively the size of an orange, had grown between her frontal and temporal lobes. When I went to the hospital to see her, a welted red zipper cut across her forehead, just below where her hair used to grow. Jenny held court in her postop room—showing off her staples, going over the details of sawing through her skull, removing her bone, sewing her scalp back on. The doctor said the surgery went well, but Jenny was irreverent, disrespectful—she didn't trust the doctors to know what they were doing. For all she knew, the surgeon might have left gauze packing in her head or stitched her up with clamps cramping her blood vessels.

Jenny.

When the bones of Jenny's skull were sawed open, she was twenty-one and technically married to a man that hit her, although she had left him and was "with" Marvin, whom she called her "husband." To Jenny, Marvin really was her husband. She didn't recognize the authority of a "stupid piece of paper" any more than she recognized the authority of a doctor. The first and last time I ever saw Marvin was at Jenny's hospital bed. I know that, compared to other men she had been with, Marvin was kind to her. But I couldn't see that. I couldn't see past his forty-year-old sun-leathered skin, past his alcoholic-sallow complexion. All I could see was Frank: an old man, with half his teeth gone, looking for something in that child's body to make him "whole." I wanted to scream, rage, hit. I wanted to throw up, moan, cry, die. I wanted to back up time, to make Jenny safe, to keep her child's body for her alone, intact.

My heart broke for her brokenness, the brokenness she'd inherited from all of us. I felt the weight of what I owed her, how much I had to make up to her. So when she said that she wanted to find Frank, that she wanted to stand in front of him and tell him what a sonofabitch he is, I said that I would help her. At that moment, I would have promised her anything, sacrificed anything I had to grant her brain-cancer wish.

Four years had passed since the haunted house threatened to swallow me up. I thought I'd made my peace with my past, with Frank, with the heartbreaking history we'd all been carrying. I thought I was "better," "healed." I had finally gotten out of a marriage that had become violent and had gotten back into school: I was starting my Ph.D. program in the fall. Three years before, when I'd struggled with whether to try to find Frank for myself, to confront him and demand an explanation, I'd decided that there was no point to it: He was who he was, and nothing I ever did could change that. I thought I was making a rational decision to get on with my life. Jenny, whose decisions were seldom rational and who wasn't sure she'd have a life to get on with, was much more honest. She wanted to look him in the eye and say, "Fuck you."

I left Jenny in her hospital room, went home, and called a private investigator. All he needed was Frank's Social Security number, a brief history, and his last known address. He discovered that Frank was being treated as an outpatient in the Oncology unit at the Rosewood clinic in Oregon. What the private investigator did not know was the date of his next appointment: I would have to find that out for myself. It seemed simple on the surface—just call the clinic, a concerned daughter who had forgotten the date of her father's next appointment. But it took me two days to move past the fear paralyzing me, and I had to practice an entire day to keep my voice from cracking, to keep my hand from shaking and dropping the phone. Finally, I did it. I found out that Frank had an appointment August 23, 1992; all I had to do was get the plane tickets and reserve the rental car, then take Jenny out to Oregon.

In late May, seven months after Jenny's surgery, I was speeding down I-75 South to Tampa while Jenny was driving north on U.S. 41, on her way home from the hospital. I was driving down to tell her that we were headed out to Oregon; she was coming home with the results of her last MRI—she was clean, her cancer was gone. Before either of us could get where we were going, a truck ran into her and cut off the top of her car. Her mangled body was rushed to the hospital, where it took four hours to catch up to her brain, which was already dead. Four hours that Margaret sat, watching her baby die.

By the time I got to Tampa, Jenny was already dead. After surviving her father, Frank, the string of men who beat her, and brain cancer, Jenny died in a car wreck before I could tell her I'd found Frank and was bringing her to Oregon.

Jenny's death was an uncanny repetition across four generations—Lily, Mother, Margaret, and Jenny. Lily was a young wife with two children when her family was in a car wreck—her husband died, and she and the children survived. Just like with my mother. Margaret and Mother were young children when they survived the crashes that took their father's lives. Jenny broke the car wreck pattern. She died.

———————

J enny died in May 1992. That fall, I got a divorce and back into graduate school. I swore I would never, ever, ever let myself be hit again, never again stay in the same house as a man who used his words or hands against me. I swore I would not live fucked-up in secret anymore. I had spent twenty-eight years of my life afraid. I had let my body be ground and blown into a looking glass that could reflect back to my father the image of himself he wanted to see. At eighteen, running away from the summer of Frank and Sally, that was all I knew how to be: a distorted mirror, reflecting back what I thought the "other" wanted to see, seeing myself twice refracted through the gaze fixing me. After Jenny died, I wanted to break myself as lying mirror. My nightmares—killing me, torturing me, breaking and shattering me—helped me do that.

As lying mirror, I failed Jenny in a hundred ways, and I was complicit in her suffering. I was complicit by being "good": As a "good" girl, I kept the secrets she was trying so hard to tell. I betrayed her by holding myself up as "good" and "together" and letting her take the rap for being "bad" and "fucked-up." What, after all, was the *difference* between Jenny and me? At eighteen, I left the summer of Frank and Sally with a man I'd just met. I stayed ten years with him, despite the fact that, when he was angry, he could call me stupid or bitch and hit me. What was the *difference* between this and Jenny, in the middle of a punch-hit-kick fight, calling me and saying, "I'd rather be fucked and then hit than not fucked at all, because the only way I know if I am loved is if I am fucked"? What was the *difference,* except that I lived fucked-up in secret? Jenny, at least, had the courage of her truth: She lived fucked-up loud and outright. Compared to Jenny, I was a liar, acquiescing to silence. When she died, I wanted to tell the *truth,* no matter what it cost.

> *I know I am romanticizing Jenny. I know it wasn't just "courage" that let her yell, fight, and live fucked up outright. I know her inability to "fit in" wasn't simply her choice, that she suffered for this. I know she envied me my ability to "pass." And I know I was not simply a "lying mirror"—that it was not my "choice" to function as mirror any more than it was Jenny's "choice" to live*

*out, publicly, the symptoms of fucked-up. I know my mirror self
let me sleep in a bed while Georgia lived under a bridge, helped
me get through college, get jobs. And I know the "truth" is not
such a simple thing, is not so easy to "know" or to "tell."*

*Knowing this doesn't change how I felt: Guilt. Blame. Shame.
Not deserving to live after Jenny died. Rage. The desire to scream:*
DO NOT JUDGE HER! YOU HAVE NO RIGHT!

Not long after Jenny died, Simon gave Margaret another shot at
being "mother." His father had finally kicked him out of the
St. Louis house for good. Simon came down to Florida, one good leg
and one crutch, moved in with Margaret, and continued drinking
himself to death. Margaret could do nothing but watch. When he was
hospitalized with failing kidneys, when he was peeing almost pure
blood, she tried to convince him to finally stop drinking, to have the
surgery that could preserve his life. But he didn't feel his life was worth
preserving. He refused the surgery, checked himself out of the hospital,
and continued his suicide by alcohol. The last time he was brought to
the emergency room, his poisoned body was so weak that he couldn't
just get up and walk out. He called Margaret, who stayed for two days
in intensive care to watch her son die a lingering death, a painful death,
the death of alcoholic-cirrhosis-liver-rotted-out, kidneys-gone, how-
did-his-body-hold-on-this-long. When he took his last breath, she was
holding his hand. Just like with Jenny.

Four years after Jenny died, I finally took that trip to Oregon. This
time all I had was an old address for a business that Frank and Sally
had started together. When I got on the plane and went in search of
Frank, I wanted to kill him.

I didn't find Frank. But I did find a half-memory, a vision making
its way up from a deep inside place in my body. It happened like this:

I found the business Frank and Sally had opened in Coos Bay,
Oregon. It was a small business selling concrete lawn ornaments. I
spent three days stalking the place, looking for Frank, but he never
showed up. Neither did Sally. I recognized Sally's son, Doug—he was

the only one working there, the one who opened in the morning and closed in the evening, the one who was clearly in charge. Finally, I approached him.

"Hi, Doug? I'm Lori, Frank's daughter. I'm looking for my father."

Doug wasn't surprised.

"I thought you looked familiar." Wary, but kind.

I hadn't seen Doug since 1982, since the summer Frank and Sally started their affair and ran off together. Thirteen years and sixty nightmare pounds later, Doug told me this story:

Frank, Sally, and Doug had been partners in this business. Frank, who had always been an angry and unpredictable man, was becoming increasingly paranoid and violent. His violence became uncontrollable in 1992, the year of Jenny's brain cancer. Doug said that my brother, Mike, told Frank that Jenny said he molested her, that she wanted to confront him, and that I was trying to find him so that I could bring her out to tell him he was a sonofabitch. One day, over a trivial thing (Doug had changed a lock or failed to change a lock, or something equally meaningless), Frank became so enraged that he took a shovel and started to beat Doug across the back with it. Sally had to take Doug to the hospital. In 1995, Doug told me that he still had pain in his back as a result of this beating.

Sally, faced with the choice between her uncle/lover and her son, finally had to choose (in a way) Doug over Frank. She put the business in Doug's name and forbid Frank from returning to it.

Doug told me that Sally and Frank continued in their relationship, but Frank was gone a lot, on hunting and fishing trips. He said that Frank believed people were out to get him, that he had to stay on the move. He always came back to Sally, though. His base camp.

A few hours after talking to Doug, I packed my suitcase and drove my rental car north on 101, up the coast, back to the airport in Eugene. On the way, my bones started sagging from the tired that had caught up with me. A tired like entropy. A tired like a hundred concrete weights pulling apart the atoms in my body. I stopped the car at the first place I could find, lay down on a bench in the sun, and went to sleep.

When I woke up, I realized I was at a place called Sea Lion Caves. I was so tired when I pulled over that I had barely registered the people milling about, the direction in which they all seemed to be headed. Disoriented—from the last three days, from the tired that I hadn't really shaken, from the nap on the bench and waking up in this place—I decided to follow these people. The Oregon landscape conjured Alaska for me, brought back the feeling of wilderness—of miles and miles of trees and mountains, glacial lakes, king salmon, buffalo in the school yard. In my dazed half-awake following-the-people state, I slipped in between times—in between this spot on the Oregon coast and the first and second grade in Alaska, summer camp on Boleo Lake, the vague half-memories I have of Frank.

I followed people to a place where we could buy tickets, followed them into an elevator with a recording that announced we would be descending 200 feet into the earth, the equivalent of twelve stories. When the elevator stopped, we got out and entered an observatory; on the other side of a glass wall, whiskers and snouts and tails and the massive expanse of bellies and backs pressed up against it, were sea lions. Sea lions and walruses. Hundreds of them. Absolutely unconcerned with the puny little humans on the other side of the glass wall, staring out at them. Unconcerned as in not bothered, not worried. We were no threat to them. But a few of them were on-and-off curious, looking back at us looking out at them. They were beyond beautiful. They were primal. Overpowering.

I was lost to them. The smell of them—primeval ocean, the life of wild, untamed things—condensed the vague memories of Alaska free-floating in me into an intense aching that traveled the perimeter of my body and then collapsed my heart into my stomach. I was a child again, flooded with sensations from the summer of '69, when we camped our way from Indiana to Alaska, through the Yukon Territory, all the way up to the land of the aurora borealis. Simultaneous with the wild smells of the walruses, I remembered the morning smells of frying bacon and coffee, the rough texture of wooden picnic benches in the campgrounds, the military-issue green poncho liners and gray wool blankets we slept with, the cigarettes and bar of chocolate in the C rations we ate.

And I had an image of Frank, tender, happy. He was opening up his military-buckled heavy-duty ice chest, sorting through containers of canned fruit, cottage cheese, the supply of C rations he always had with him. He was distributing this food carefully, like presents, cautiously, to make it last. A slight intake of breath, a catching sound in his throat, accompanied his handing-around-the-food motions. This buckled metal box was his treasure chest, the magic metal that held cold and preserved food, that fed us on those trips from duty station to duty station.

This image of Frank tending his ice chest conflated with Frank, driven, driving us. I remembered those long stretches of time when Frank drove straight through the night, drove and drove and drove until he was too tired to push his body any more, and we could stop, finally, at one of the highway rest areas where we so frequently slept. At two and three in the morning, we would sprawl across picnic tables and benches or hunch in the back seat of the car, hunkering down for whatever sleep we could get. When Frank had had whatever kind of respite his body needed to get us on the road again, we pushed our cramped bodies into upright car-riding positions and started waiting, again, for the end of the road.

The Oregon coastline and sea lion caves brought all this back to me: Alaska, Frank always hunting or fishing, elk and moose and caribou, animal traps in the basement with their steel claws and death-knell hinges. And this image of Frank hit me, left me winded: Frank, as a tortured animal caught in one of those steel traps, severing his own body on the metal jaws he was trying to wrench himself free of, licking-biting his punctured flesh, trying to claw-eat his way out of a trap that, on one side, is wide open. If he could just stop, calm himself, look around, he could back up, exit the trap intact.

I never found Frank. But, from the promontory overlooking the Pacific Ocean, I found an aching kind of sorrow for Frank's wounds, for his wounding. A sorrow that cried for Simon and Jenny, dead; for Sandra and Marnie, lost to Margaret; for all the ways that the wounds we do not tend repeat themselves, over and over again.

9

IF OUR FIRST LANGUAGE
IS THE SILENCE OF COMPLICITY,
HOW DO WE LEARN TO SPEAK?

April 2001

Standing in the O'Hare airport, tears dripping down my chin, onto my shirt, can't stop them. Surrounded by teenagers, eighteen- and nineteen-year-old naval recruits, just out of basic training at the Naval Training Center in Chicago. They're in their dress blues, bent under the weight of their duffle bags. Pimples. They look scared. Confused. How many of these kids are poor, from small towns? Kids who enlisted in the navy because it looked like a way "out"? Out of poverty, out of dead-end small towns with no jobs for them? How many of them are trading three years of their lives for a shot at the college money their recruiters promised them?

They're so young! Just babies! Half these boys don't even need to shave. The girls, hair short or in knots at the base of their skulls, looking like they got lost in the army-navy surplus store. These kids, lost in a big-city airport, bumbling around under their duffle bags, looking scared and confused—we're putting guns in their hands, telling them to shoot? What are we doing? What's our definition of a child soldier? Thirteen? Fourteen? What makes eighteen the magic number?

Yesterday, I was at the Adams Mark Hotel, talking to an audience of college professors about how to craft writing assignments that allow students to research and write about traumas they have had in their lives. I was telling them it can be healing, that some students will take the opportunity of their college writing classes to begin to work through the old wounds they carry. I believed it then, believe it now. I did it. My college classes helped me find a way to live beyond the wounding Frank brought home with him. But here, in this airport, my heart breaking for these babies who have just spent six weeks on shooting ranges and physical training, I despair. How can the handful of students working with the handful of professors who try to make college classrooms a place of personal growth and healing ever keep pace with all these babies we dress up as soldiers, arm with guns, wound, and send out to make more wounding in the world?

I was twenty-one the first time I stood up to Frank. I was in my last semester of my undergraduate degree at the University of Hawaii, taking an independent study in feminist theory with my mentor, Cristina Bacchilega. I had switched my major from philosophy to English, partly because of Cristina. She was kind to me. She encouraged me, motivated me, inspired me. I had always had a fantasy about going to graduate school, but Cristina was helping me make that fantasy real. With her, I was reading Virginia Woolf, Sandra Gilbert, Susan Gubar, and Helene Cixous. She was showing me how to write the kind of paper that would be required of me in a graduate program.

Cristina was working on her own research that semester, and she let me come to her house for our meetings. At her house, I saw a world I wanted to inhabit: a love of learning, a kind heart, a commitment to making a better world. She was helping me imagine what kind of person I wanted to be.

This was not an easy imagining. I was still waking up at night, crying, my guilt and my shame eating away at me. I cried for my mother, living alone in a falling-apart trailer in Davenport, Florida. I cried over my guilt for protecting Frank, for lying for him and helping keep his secrets. In the summer of 1985, studying feminist theorists by day and crying at night, I finally found the courage to call my father and tell him that I would not keep his secrets anymore. When I spoke, finally, the violence of his rage terrified me.

————————

July 1985—Journal Entry

Called Frank. Told him I couldn't lie for him anymore, that what he is doing is wrong. That he has a financial responsibility to Mother, that he abandoned her in that campground, humiliated her, that he owes her better. I told him that his affair with Sally is wrong, that I can't keep that secret anymore. She is his niece. He screamed at me, cussed. He called me cunt and slut. He said he sacrificed his life for me, and I have betrayed him. He said he would kill Mother, that he would leave her dead, in a gutter, and it would be my fault, all my fault. I was crying. I yelled back at him—I told him he was wrong, asked how could he say he would kill people, what is wrong with him? I don't remember everything—he told me never to call him again, that he would kill us all if I tried to find him. Black fog, numb. Crying so long my whole body tired from it. Don't know how my skin keeps from splitting apart. Guilt, rage. On the phone, I begged him—stop, please, Daddy, take it back, say you don't mean it, say you are sorry.

This phone conversation with Frank was a turning point. It was the first time since he told me about his affair with Sally that I could say, no, this is wrong. I cannot lie for you anymore. You are making me complicit, and I will no longer be your accomplice. But it took three years and a professor who showed me another way to live in the world before I could say, "I will not keep your secret anymore."

In the summer of 1985, my middle-of-the-night crying and my work with Cristina were slowly opening a path through the paralysis of my silences. When I was finally able to speak—to say, "I will not keep your secrets anymore," and "I will not be complicit"—the violent force of Frank's rage severed all communication between us. For

As for my health it is far from good but I dont burden any one with my problems,

Aside from diabetes, a pacemaker pulmonary embolus and cancer of the eye I am fine.

Though a heart attack and cancer surgery on my eye I have never even received a get well card from any of you. As long as I live I wont bother any one for I dont have to take these insults and ignorant abuse.

I spent all of my life doing for all of you and I do love each and every one even the girls I was told werent mine. You have your hurts and I damn sure have mine.

Dont tell me again it is what I want for you damn well arent interested in knowing what I want or how I feel.

Only ▒▒▒▒ and Little ▒▒▒▒ ever contact me and if that is the way it must be then so be it I detest your lily white perfectness and one day you will see it.

Excerpt from Frank's June 15, 1985, letter.

two years, I did not hear from him. The phone number I had for him was disconnected.

————————

Two years later, I talked to Frank one last time. Mother had wrecked the Toyota Corolla that I left her when I went to New York; she was hurt, and the car was totaled. She was in Florida, alone, injured, without a car. I was in California, working on my master's thesis in English at the University of California in San Diego, broke, a working college student. Zane and Mike were the most help to Mother; they gave her money every month, fixed the trailer, took care of her problems. I had used all the money I made from my jobs to stay in college, spent all the time I was not at work or in classes on my private dramas. I was guilty and angry, and I wanted Frank to give Mother the help that I could not.

So I called Sally's ex-husband, Douglas, to see if he knew where Frank and Sally were. He did not—they kept where they lived a secret from him too. But he said his kids, Kendall and Melissa, were in touch with Sally, and they might be able to help me. Douglas gave me Kendall's number. Kendall and Melissa, it turned out, were in San Diego, going to San Diego State University. They were right here, in the same city where I was. I called Kendall and told him about the car wreck, that I needed to find Frank, that Mother needed help. Kendall told me he would call Sally and get the message to Frank.

November 1987: Frank Calls

In my composition and rhetoric class tonight, having the under-water feeling again—hovering beneath the surface, looking up at the people floating above me, colored specs bumper-carring into one another. It's the fog thing that happens—people talk-ing, but I don't really know what they are saying. I am agitated, waiting for class to end.

Finally, class over—9:30 by the time I am driving home. It is dark, not cold, but chilly. The drive back to the apartment is bleak. Past the strip joints on El Cajon Boulevard, military crew cuts filing in and out of the doors, neon signs advertising "all-nude." I get home, and the message light is flashing on the answering machine. It is Frank. His voice is angry. He says Kendall called, asks what I am doing hunting him down. He doesn't leave a number. I am afraid of his voice, but afraid with my body rising up against the fear, adrenalin spiked, primal instincts, hair on end. A freezing response, sniffing-listening-looking-sensing, muscles and nerves tensed.

I stay this way, clenched-up, for over an hour. Finally, the phone rings—it is him. He is angry, asks me what I want. I tell him about the accident. I want him to get Mother a car. I tell him that Zane and Mike have been supporting her, helping her, that I don't have any money, that we can't afford a car for Mother. I say he owes her. He says:

You are all ungrateful. I have sacrificed my life for you, and for what? You have abandoned me, all of you. Nobody calls me, nobody keeps in contact with me. Nobody cares about me. I have done everything for you, everything, and you are all selfish, ungrateful. What do you want from me? Leave me alone, leave me in peace. I wish there was a war, any war, I just want to be back in a firefight, killing gooks. Just leave me alone, goddammit, just leave me alone, all of you. If you can't leave me alone, I'll kill myself. That's what you want, isn't it? That will make you happy?

Fuck you, fuck all of you, you ungrateful bastards, I won't kill myself, I won't give you that satisfaction, you won't win—I will go on, alone, without any of you, goddammit. I have sacrificed myself my whole life for you, given you everything, and for what? I won't get her a car, goddammit, she can rot in Hell, all of you can go to Hell. What do you want from me? Haven't I given you enough? I am old and alone, with cancer and diabetes, and none of you care, none of the children. I sacrificed everything for you, and you have abandoned me, don't care whether I live or die. Go to Hell, all of you—go to Hell, goddammit! Leave me alone, don't call me again—go to Hell, all of you.

I love each of you the same but honey you have been a special comfort to me for the past seven years. You have been a joy of my life for ninteen years but as I said a special comfort the past seven years.

I have failed in this area and I have shown a weakness never before seen in me. No one has bothered to call and see how I am accepting you being gone but I did not expect them to. I guess I should appologize to you for being such a total failure as a father and for not being a stronger person. But my little one I have stood all my life and fought for what I beleived was right. I now sit here writing you in total defeat.

I have spent many a year alone and away from all of you. But today has been one of the hardest days of my entire life. What I need is a good fire fight but we have no war going on so I guess that is out. But no matter as I have been told I am to old and to sick they dont want me. One of my problems has always been is I cant quit and give in. I refuse to submit to this sickness and I refuse to just give up. I am eaither going to beat it or it will get me but not without a fight.

Excerpt from Frank's August 22, 1982, letter.

As I reconstruct this scene, using twenty-year-old journal entries, I feel the paralysis of that old emotion tugging on me. Even now, from the distance of twenty years and the safety of a tenure-track university job, with the armor of an education, knowing better, I feel the trap of his self-pity. The way it snakes around and inside me, making me responsible for the wounds he bleeds all over me. Do you hear him, in the silence of the night, telling his children all that he sacrifices for us? Do you feel him, handing his suffering to us, a gag that chokes our words back, the rope that binds our limbs, still, while he relieves himself of his suffering, quiet, silent, do not tell, Frank's wounds, bleeding?

———

The silence of complicity is a thick, heavy, suffocating shroud winding around and around me. It is a confusion, an incomprehension. It is a paralysis, a blindness, a blank space. It takes the physical force of a subterranean movement to break through this shroud of silence. Like the words coming out of me at Cristina's kitchen table, when I couldn't talk about *Justine*. Like the force of the haunted house caving in on me, like my floating self in the corner of the ceiling looking down at my crying body. Most important, it requires somebody to whom, or on whose behalf, to speak. If I had not had to explain my crying to Cristina, would any words have disturbed this heavy silence? If I had been alone at Mother's trailer, if Denise had not been there, would I have been able to break through this fog?

It was my body, splitting off from itself, shaking, crying, leaking words out, that broke through the weight of silence. But it was through my witnesses that I learned how to speak. My first words were accidents, marked by fear, confusion, the feeling that I had done something wrong, something bad was going to happen. Stumbling, stuttering words, mispronounced, words I wanted to take back as soon as they were out of my mouth. Like in 1988, when I was teaching high school and too afraid to sleep and taking Xanax to keep the haunted house from swallowing me up. I accidentally blurted out the truth of Frank.

———

A Rupture: Spring 1988

It was the last few weeks of the school year, which, in a small rural Florida school, meant May heat and picking the watermelon crops and cutting classes to go to the Springs. In the last period of a hot May day, in a 1950s building with a window air conditioner that noisily fanned the heat around our classroom, Lisa asked, "Ms. Amy, what's wrong? You look tired."

Before I knew what had happened, I heard myself saying, in as calm a voice as I could muster, "I've been trying to find my father, Lisa, and I haven't gotten much sleep."

Lisa, whose family was "from Trenton"—from Trenton in that way in which people and land and history are all knotted up, and you cannot separate the people from the place or vice versa—could not quite figure what it meant to have to "find" a father. So she asked, and I told her my father had been violent, had disappeared several years ago, and was keeping his whereabouts a secret. I immediately regretted my words: I thought I had done a terrible thing, that I had violated these students by contaminating them with the shame instilled in me, injured them by speaking this truth of which I was still so afraid. I wanted to protect them—protect them from the truth of myself, from the truth of my father, from the truth of these things in the world.

After class that day, after all the students had emptied out of the classrooms and hallways, Beth came back to the classroom to talk to me. She said she wanted to thank me for telling them about my father, and she began to tell me about her cousin raping her. She said she had never told anyone besides her mother before, and she was telling me now only because I had told them about my father, and she knew I would understand. She was twelve years old when her cousin raped her, violently. Crying, in pain, she went to her mother for comfort. Her mother was angry with her, ashamed.

Her words to Beth: "What did you do to provoke him?" Beth's mother slapped her and told her to never, ever let anything like this happen again.

Beth didn't really "cry" when she told me about being raped by her cousin—not the violent, sobbing, dramatic crying of movie scenes. She teared up, much like I had at Cristina's kitchen table. No sounds. A crying swallowed. Wetness trickling down a cheek, after school let out on a hot May day. When she went outside to talk to her friends in the everything-is-fine way, they would think her face was damp with Florida sweat.

I wish I could remember what I said to her. I cannot. I can remember what I felt, though: guilty, as though I had opened up a hole in the universe, and we were all going to fall through it. Afraid, as though I had done something wrong and terrible, and there was no going back. Confused. I know I did not have anything to "offer" Beth—no help, no comfort, nothing that could take her pain away or make up for what she had suffered.

In the years since that first accidental, inappropriate blurting out loud, I have come to understand how our speaking can help others. That day, I did not "understand" anything. What I "understood" was that I was fighting off crazy and I might contaminate my students, hurt them with the hurting Frank left in me. Fortunately, I had Kathrin to help me—Kathrin, who, once a week, sat with me while I cried out my shame, who helped me find my way through panic attacks and nightmares, and who helped me find the courage and the skill to go back into the classroom and use my inappropriate blurting out loud as a teaching tool, a way of looking honestly at ourselves and our world.

The day Beth knelt beside me and told me about her cousin, though, I did not know how to do any of that. I did not "help" Beth. I could hold onto the story that Beth's words gave me—that speaking about my father gave her an opening to tell the heavy secret she had been carrying. I could stop there. But this scene is much more complicated than that. Was Beth's speaking not a way of responding to the hurting-pain-shame she read in me, an attempt to take care of me? Reaching out to say, "It's okay. Look, me too. You are not alone. You did not hurt us. See, here, look, I know what you are feeling"?

I do not think Beth had any more "conscious" control over her speaking than I did over mine. I think her words were the unconscious response of a tenth-grade girl who knew too much about the hurting of this world—for both of us, speaking as an upheaval of the body, words wrenching their way through the physical weights of fear, denial, confusion, doubt.

I did not know, then, what to do with these words, with the rupturing of this speech.

A Mirror: Fall 1988

In the fall of 1988, I had a class of eleventh graders to whom I was supposed to be teaching American literature. They were the vocational track kids, kids who did not like school and who liked literature even less, kids who called themselves, with the pride of appropriation, "sweat hogs." I was not mature enough or skilled enough to know how to do a good job with them.

It was a fluke that I ever got that job teaching high-school English in the first place. The summer of '87, when Lewis was undergoing psychiatric evaluation for his sleep walking and increasing violence, it was clear he was going to be discharged from the navy. I had to throw myself on the mercy of my teachers at the University of California at San Diego to organize a thesis committee, take thesis hours over the summer, speed up my work so that I could graduate in December. Lewis was discharged late that summer, and I got a job working full-time as a proofreader at a law firm while I finished my course work and my thesis. In December, we moved to Gainesville, Florida, partly because my brother Leonard was there and partly because the University of Florida had a nuclear reactor at which Lewis thought he might be able to work. In January 1988, I was looking for any kind of work I could get. Besides applying at Trenton High School, I had applied to wait tables at the Holiday Inn. Trenton called first. A teacher had left in the middle of the year, and the school needed an emergency replacement. I had a master's degree, but no teacher training.

I was all they had. They were all I had. They hired me, and I was grateful. Stupid, young, unprepared—but grateful. Within four months of starting the job, I was taking Xanax to ward off panic attacks and fighting the ghosts of the past that was trailing me. I spent the summer of 1988 trying to understand these ghosts and taking education classes to learn how to be a "good" teacher. By the time school started in August, I was armed with my Xanax, theories of "classroom management," and strategies for "taking control" of unruly students. My grip on both my ghosts and theories of classroom control was tenuous at best. Jimmy, barging in late to our second-period American literature class, made me lose my hold of both of them.

I was scared of the second-period students—mostly boys, rough, rowdy. They spent most of their day in auto mechanic and woodworking classes. Half of them had failed one or more grades. They were between seventeen and nineteen years old, only a few years younger than I was, but more than a foot taller. I was twenty-five, almost five foot two, and

I had not yet gained the sixty pounds that would come from trying to shut up my nightmares. I looked like my students. I used all the strategies from my summer teacher training with these boys who made me afraid. I had work ready for them when they walked into the room. I offered no "unorganized" time, no time that was not "on task," during which, bored or irritable, they would have an opportunity to "make trouble." I was firm. "In control." When Jimmy barged in, late, with "attitude," I asked him, "Why are you late?" Tardies, according to the principles of classroom management, "are not allowed." To keep students orderly, on task, disciplined, tardies must be discouraged. Some teachers said tardy students must be "punished," and Trenton High School did, indeed, punish students. Sending teenagers to the office to be paddled was routine practice. I objected to this and refused to send my students to the office to be hit. Instead, I developed my own system of after-school detention. Jimmy, who was absent a lot and tardy again, was headed for detention.

Jimmy was unimpressed with my strategies for managing the class. He threw his books down, called me a bitch, and hurled his six-foot-plus body through the door and out of the room.

I did not know, when Jimmy called me a bitch and fled from the class, what made the rage screaming through his body. But the absurdity of it—throwing his books, calling me a bitch—stopped me in my tracks. The absurdity and the violence. I froze. Just froze. Did not move. I had no words. Into the vacuum of this frozen-in-place confusion, students began speaking. They speculated that Jimmy's parents were fighting again, that somebody had beaten him. They said that he had been sleeping in his car. His house was a place of fighting-yelling-screaming-cussing-hurting, and, when he went back there, a fight broke out—a physical fight, with family members beating each other.

I do not know what students in that class felt as they were talking about Jimmy and what he was living through. I do not know if they felt, in their bodies, the *shame* that Jimmy must endure. But I felt it. Listening to them, the heat of my own shame began melting the fear that had frozen me in place. I felt as though I knew Jimmy, as though I knew his desperate desire to be loved, knew the rage and shame that come with feeling abandoned, unloved, alone in the world. The force of this shame hit me like a physical blow.

In the fall of 1988, when Jimmy threw down his books and called me a bitch, I did not understand what was happening. I did not "think." I did not know enough to realize that his behavior was disproportionate to the situation, that his rage had to be about something else, that it was triggered by asking him why he was late. I did not consciously understand, then, how to deescalate potentially violent situations. I just froze, trapped inside of the old fear response Frank wrote into me. Nor did I choose the pity that flooded me as students began talking about the violence in his family. My urgent desire to ease the burden of the shame I imagined Jimmy carrying, to open up a space for his dignity, was as much a product of the scripts I had learned from Frank as was the fear that had paralyzed me.

I acted from my pity. Later that day, when I found Jimmy, I said the only thing I could think of. I said, "I am sorry. I didn't know. Is there anything I can do?"

He was angry, hurting, shamed. He was dirty, and he smelled. He felt no hope, did not trust me, rebuffed me. I was awkward, stumbling, at a loss. I had no more "help" for him than I had for Beth. Between us, we had bodies in turmoil, an emotional flooding that could not find its words.

Nothing was "resolved" in that conversation. There was no "healing" or hope or happy ending. After that, though, Jimmy was a "good" student in my class. Not in terms of reading, or studying, or doing well on tests. But he came, and he behaved well, and his good behavior made other students behave better. In a class of mostly boys, the vocational nonacademic track, the "problem" kids, Jimmy set a standard for "good" behavior that the rest of the students followed.

Occasionally, he would come by my room to talk to me—after school, at lunch. Sometimes, he would skip class and come to my planning period. Mostly, he talked about what made him angry, who hurt him, who he wanted to hurt back. I had nothing to give him but my pity. I did not know how to help him. He was seventeen-turning-eighteen in the eleventh grade; as soon as his birthday came, he dropped out of school and joined the marines. I got a letter from him a year or so after he left. It was short, not much detail. He wanted me to know he was doing okay.

I did the tiniest, smallest little thing. Instead of punishing Jimmy for his outburst, instead of meeting his violent eruption with greater violence of my own, I said, "I am sorry. I didn't know. Is there anything I can do?" As a result, Jimmy changed his behavior with me. It was the tiniest, smallest little thing. It did not make him a "good boy" in his other classes, did not change anything in his family, did not stop him from going into the marines and making a living out of the hitting-screaming-yelling-fighting that he grew up in.

I still think about Jimmy, Beth, Lisa—all the students who taught me. It is not too much to say that I "love" them. Love like gratitude, compassion. Love like a mirror that shows me what I cannot see in myself, by myself. Love like the guideposts that point, not to the destination, but at least to the direction for a future. My students teach me that living differently is a possibility. And they give me the responsibility of looking for this different way, even when—especially when—I lose my own capacity for hope.

10

THE WORK OF WAR

If you are exposed to violence, you become violent. And this is a fact of life, not a fact solely of war. The war may come to a formal end, but all those people who have learned violence—learned to solve their problems, and conflicts, and confusions with violence—will continue to use it. They will be more violent with their families, with their friends, in their work. They will see violence as the appropriate response to any political contest. . . . Violence lives in the belly of the person and ruins society, unless peace is taught to the violent. And peace must be taught just like violence is, by subjecting people to it, by showing them peaceful ways to respond to life and living, to daily needs and necessities, to political and personal challenges. (Nordstrom 2004, 180)

People don't simply kill or not kill, torture or not torture. A vast and complicated set of beliefs and values must be in place to determine (and justify) who may and may not be killed, how they may be harmed, by whom, and under what conditions. (Nordstrom 2004, 154)

January 2002

In the bathroom in Newton Building. Can't stop crying. Prisoners in Guantánamo Bay. George W. Bush says that these are not human beings, not prisoners of war—calls them "enemy combatants," says that Geneva Rights do not apply. We are torturing them. I know we are torturing them. I feel myself ripping open, a burning in my vagina. It is all I can do to keep from doubling over. I can't stop crying, bordering hysterical. Getting dizzy, my head going black.

Marge comes in, asks me what is wrong. I tell her: We're torturing these people. Snot runs down my nose, and I try to wipe it off. Marge looks at me like I'm crazy. I cry to her, say that I should have gone to work with Amnesty International, shouldn't be here, shouldn't be letting this happen—have to do something to stop it, we have to stop this, we can't let it happen.

"You don't really think they're torturing anybody, do you? Surely, we wouldn't do that!"

Is she crazy? How can she say that?

"What do you think that saying 'They're not prisoners of war. They are enemy combatants' means? Why do you think we're saying that the rights established at the Geneva Conventions don't apply? *What do you think this means??*"

I'm raising my voice, I know I am. I try to stop, to bring myself under control. I have to teach. I'm in public, on my university campus. Thank God it's Marge, not somebody who would call—who would she call? Who would somebody call to say that I'm in the bathroom, verging on hysterical, sobbing, out of control?

"Maybe this will be over quickly. It won't go on too long," she says.

Breathe, I have to breathe. Take deep breaths. Hold for ten. Exhale, slowly—another ten count. Ten of these. Cold water on my face.

Later, talking to my friend Angela. Who knows, like I know, that we are torturing prisoners. Who does not need words to explain this. Who knows the incoherence of words in the face of this. Who does not look at me as though I'm crazy.

She tells me that Marge told her she saw me in the bathroom.

I ask: How can Marge not understand that we are torturing people?

Her first eight years, Angela was raised in South Africa. During Apartheid. Under a regime. When her mother had her memorize books from the Bible in case they were arrested. In case they were tortured.

Angela says, "The question is not 'How can Marge not know that people are being tortured?' Normal people wouldn't know that. The question is 'How do *you* know?'"

How do we know what we know? And what do we know that we do not know that we know? How is it that I have this dizziness, this blackness, this hysteria, upon reading that we are denying Geneva Rights to "enemy combatants" in Guantánamo Bay? How is it that I feel, in my body, what is being done?

Is it because of the basement in Alaska? Where Frank kept his animal traps? Big traps, bigger than me. Traps for moose, elk, caribou.

Frank moved us to Alaska shortly after he got back from Vietnam. The summer between kindergarten and my first "real" grade in school, he requested a tour of duty at Fort Greely, a small army base in Alaska's subarctic circle. Fort Greely is the army's "Northern Warfare Training Center." This means that people go there to freeze their asses off and maybe almost die to gain the glorious title of "One Who Battles Cold and Conquers Mountains." It is also the place where the army tests equipment for arctic conditions—bombs, tanks, helicopters, and the like—as part of their arctic war survival training. It is called the "Home of the Rugged Professional"—so isolated, so remote, so harshly cold, that it is considered "overseas" duty. This is where Frank moved us as soon as he got back from Vietnam.

The distance between the jungles of Southeast Asia and the subarctic circle is closed by this: Frank's body, waging a war against its own vulnerability. Fight the "gooks" and nature and survive Korea, Vietnam. Fight Alaska, the wilderness, big game. Fight the "enemy"— the Koreans or the Japs or the hippies and niggers and commies. Fight everything, all the time—fight, fight, fight. And underneath it all, this war against the fragility, the vulnerability, of his own body.

This, I think, is the war he fought, over and over again—a war he could never win.

Other things were in that basement besides the animal traps. My sister Georgia tells this story: She was in the basement, and she found one of those old viewfinder toys, popular in the '70s, the little handheld picture viewers, with binocular-like lenses that you held up to your eyes and a disc of 3D photographic images that you flipped through by moving a lever that advanced the film. She looked through it and saw women—when she told me the story, she called them "Oriental"—who were naked. Who were posed. Who were being fucked. Hit. Beaten. Bleeding. Tied up. Cut.

I hold these images together with the spring of 1991, just after the first Persian Gulf War, when I was teaching at Trenton High School.

April 1991

I try to keep my students from going to the auditorium. I heard about it during third period—that Todd's stepfather had come back from Kuwait, where his reserve unit had been deployed during the Persian Gulf War, with pictures. He has these pictures displayed in the auditorium, and students have been going in all day to look at them. Photographs of dead Iraqis—limbs missing, blood everywhere. I can't believe the high school principal let him bring these pictures to school, set up a public display. I can't believe this school is sending students in to look, with pride, at pictures of dead Iraqis. The boys come back from the auditorium, euphoric, happy, proud. This could be a football game that they have just won. They say, "We kicked ass." "That'll teach 'em." "Towel Heads." "Sand Niggers." "Nuke 'em all."

I don't know where Todd's stepfather got these pictures. I don't think he "fought," don't think he was one of the people who dropped bombs. He was in a reserve unit, mostly in Kuwait. What were they doing over there?

What are we doing to these boys? They are children—fourteen, fifteen, sixteen—they don't even shave! And these words are coming out of their mouths, dehumanizations, obscenities. They are learning to forget that these are human beings they are looking at. They are learning to make killing abstract, to associate pride and pleasure with images of dead bodies. This is obscene, sick. It is sick, sick, sick—how can the school *do* this?

There should be somebody I can call. Isn't there somebody I can *call?* Can this be *legal?* This school is teaching these boys how to hate, how to split themselves off from themselves and deny the humanity they share with the Iraqis who were killed in this war. They are learning how to deny the pain, terror, carnage that these pictures show. *How can they do this? How can I let this happen?*

I did protest. I told my students: This is wrong. This war, these deaths, these things are cause for grief, for mourning, not for celebration. I told the principal these pictures should not be displayed. I had my students watch the news, explained to them the history of the 1980s, when the United States was funding Saddam Hussein and building his army. I tried to give them some of the historical context of which they were completely ignorant—about the Shah of Iran, the revolution and the Ayatollah Ruholla Khomeini, the Iran-Iraq war. My students told their parents what I told them. Their parents complained to the principal. The principal told me not to talk about the war anymore.

Amnesia. Denial. A blind patriotism that, in its blindness, loves killing.

So how could I have been surprised when, in 2001, almost all the students in my university classes knew the last contestants on a popular reality show, but not one of them had heard of the Patriot Act? And even most of the professors with whom I worked were not questioning who we were arresting in our "war on terror," on what evidence, what it meant to label these people "enemy combatants" and deny them the rights established at the Geneva Conventions.

Silence, denial, the work of forgetting and the making of scapegoats—these are the fabric of our daily lives.

And now we have Abu Ghraib.

But we have always had Abu Ghraibs. Priscilla Hayner, in her work on the Truth and Reconciliation Commissions,[1] provides precise accounts of the American military's participation in torture—training other countries' militaries in interrogation techniques, backing regimes and insurgencies and counter-insurgencies, supplying arms and equipment, assisting and overseeing, witnessing. Nor is Abu Ghraib the first place where pictures were taken—somebody's documentation, somebody's record, somebody's pleasure. For historians who know how and where to look, our century provides too many instances, too much evidence of our torture.

---

1 In countries that have been torn apart by civil wars—in South America, Africa, Yugoslavia—International Commissions investigating the crimes committed have been established to help forge postconflict peace. The most famous is South Africa's Truth and Reconciliation Commission. For more information, see Hayner 2002.

All these instances, all this evidence, on a continuum with a view-finder in a basement in Alaska and Todd's father displaying pictures of dead Iraqis in a high-school auditorium.

But Abu Ghraib became public, in this age of digital cameras and CDs and the Internet. Many of those photos have made their way into a particular subculture of Internet pornography. This event-ness of Abu Ghraib—the public exposure of this torture, met in some quarters with outrage, in others with denial, appropriated into the excesses of a pornographic culture, beg us to ask: What does the brutal horror of the sexualized torture committed by average-Jane and average-Joe American soldiers tell us about the psychic mutilations that make "man" and "woman" in this world? About the psychic mutilations that make and are fed by our wars?

The first question I ask: Why *these* acts? Why stage torture as sadistic pornography, obscene? What fantasy is behind this? But then I have to ask: Is not all torture, no matter its staging, obscene? At its root, is torture a thing of the sexual body that has been twisted, mutilated? Is the blade that cuts always a version of a penetration, slicing through the hymen of the skin separating inside from outside? The naked body. The cut, the bleeding. Beating, ripping skin, breaking bone. Rape. Burning and electrocuting genitals. Sodomizing victims, forcing victims to rape and sodomize each other.

What about all the beatings adults give children? Mike and Georgia, beaten. All those years, Frank's body, erupting. Is this, too, part of the perversion of his sex, his body erupting and spewing itself onto his victims? The tension knotting his muscles, racing his heart, oxygen and blood flooding his major muscle groups. His throbbing body bursting open onto the bodies of his children. His lunging body thrusting fists, feet, spasming, until he reaches his climax, draining the fury of his racing heart, pumping blood, hardened muscles.

Of all the photos from Abu Ghraib, the one that most haunts me is this: an Iraqi man, a black hood on his head, naked from his waist down, forced onto the floor, on his side, hands cuffed behind his back. In this position—with his hands manacled, arms wrenched behind his back—American soldiers make him open his buttocks, insert a banana into his anus. Why this image? Of all of the horrifying images documenting the American occupation of Iraq, why is it this picture of torture that haunts me?

There is so much to be haunted by. More than six hundred thousand Iraqis dead. The horrifying devastation of the country—the daily bombing of houses, the kidnappings, shootings, no electricity or water in many places, life reduced to a search for water, food, for loved ones who are missing, the tally of who has died today, the often futile attempt to recover the bodies of the dead, to give them burials when possible. Gunfire the new music in the streets, fear a constant presence. Hatred building, against the helplessness, humiliation, degradation that life has become.

These horrors—day to day, multiplied by millions—are on a continuum with Abu Ghraib—part of the fabric of violence that has taken over daily life. And these horrors are not hidden, are not carried on in secret. They are reported—we can read about them in newspapers, in magazines, in the hundreds of blogs and online media available to anybody with an Internet connection.

These are horrors that, perfectly visible to us, we choose not to see. And, when we do see them, we either numb ourselves, desensitized, nonresponsive to something far away, not fully real to us, or we deny the truth of the reports that seep through our commercialized, propagandized, nationalized media.

The language that saturates us—the language of a "war on terror" and "axis of evil"—is a language of death. It creates the Iraqi civilian—the ordinary man, the ordinary woman, the ordinary child, the six hundred thousand victims of these seven years of war—as an "enemy," a "threat," a "terrorist." This is the first and most fundamental work of war: the creation of an "enemy" against whom we direct our fear, whom we blame for all that we suffer.

Perfectly visible but disavowed, we apply the work of forgetting to the everyday horror that has become life in Iraq. This work of forgetting is part of what makes and allows Abu Ghraib. But this image of torture that haunts me is a part of this work of forgetting too. It functions as a screen, concealing as much as it reveals. Exposing the sexual violation of a male body, it conceals what this war is doing to women. We will never know the extent of the violence inflicted on

Iraqi women—most of them would rather die than speak of what has been done to them.

Despite the secrecy, the cover-ups, the impossibility of knowing about most of the violence that is committed, a few of the worst crimes become public. These few—the very, very few that the general public hears about—are still too many to keep count of. The rampant rapes of townswomen by soldiers—as in March 2006, when U.S. soldiers killed Abeer Qassim Hamza's mother, father, and five-year-old sister, then raped and killed her.[2] Then there are all the rapes that come with sectarian violence, with the rise in fundamentalism and restrictions on women that accompany the breakdown of economic and political structures through these long years of military occupation. And, too, there are the American women, raped by soldiers with whom they serve. Or dead, dehydrated because they were afraid to drink water too late in the day—to drink water risks having to make a trip to the latrines in the middle of the night, when they would be easy targets for men in their units.

So many people are victims of the brutality of this war, so many women and children who will remain invisible, anonymous, whose traumas will never register in our collective consciousness. Does this image haunt me because the form the torture takes calls up the ghosts of all the people whose suffering we will never see?

The horror of this image is manifold, multilayered. It exposes other acts that we do not notice, that we take for granted. For instance, this image mimes the genre of pornography that has women fuck themselves—dildos, masturbation, objects, animals—to satisfy a particular kind of male sexual fantasy that is common, that remains unremarked. This image mirrors pornographic e-mail that I have received, in the days before pop-up blockers could prevent spam messages from automatically opening up on our computer screens. In one of these e-mails, three women were posed on their hands and knees, buttocks displayed for the camera, faces invisible. A man's groin, shot in profile, showed an erect penis ready to penetrate the exposed buttocks. The caption for the image read, "See huge cock rip open tight teenage ass."

---

2 For more information about this issue, see Wikipedia, "Abeer Qassim Hamza al-Janabi," and Associated Press 2006.

Internet pornography, bulk mail of the digital age, spam. The Abu
Ghraib photographs.

This image distills to its essence the psychic mutilation upon which
all our notions of "masculine" and "feminine" are based. The horror
this image of torture evokes in me is a horror that reflects, through the
violence inflicted on this man's body, the routine, day-to-day violences
that make up our lives. It lays bare the violence of a masculinity that is
defined as the negation of all that is feminine.

> *The most extreme degradation imaginable: to make a man
> a "woman."*
>
> *To penetrate, to fuck, to rape him.*
>
> *To render him passive, powerless against the to-be-fucked of
> this torture.*
>
> *Even worse, to make him make himself a "woman," to fuck
> himself, degrade and humiliate himself.*
>
> *If the torturer is a man, does making the prisoner fuck him-
> self preserve the fantasy of his own "masculinity"? If the torturer
> touches the prisoner's body—his skin, his anus, his penis—does
> he have to think, "I have sexual desire here; my erection is for this
> man"? If he touches him, penetrates him, does he have to con-
> front, differently, his own homosexual element? If he makes the
> prisoner act out his fantasy for him, does that shield him from
> his own tortured desire, let him hide from the part of himself that
> wants to fuck another man?*
>
> *What if the torturer is a woman? And it could be—women
> are there, in the photos, smiling, gloating over the sadistic sex-
> ual torture American soldiers are performing. If the torturer is
> a woman, is she getting revenge? Making a man do to himself
> what men do to women—fuck them, rape them? Is she perform-
> ing her boyfriend's desire for him? Is she using this prisoner as a
> scapegoat, one who carries all the sins for which she can hold no
> one else accountable?*

That viewfinder. Those images from Abu Ghraib.

This idea of a "man" is the foundational fantasy upon which all our
social and cultural structures depend. Our religions, our families, our

governments, our militaries—all are built on a twisted, distorted, split-down-the-middle fantasy of "man" that makes "woman" its opposite. To be a man, you have to kill any traces of what is "woman" in you—what is weak, tender, vulnerable, emotional. And to prove yourself a man, after killing all that is woman within you, you have to conquer women in the world around you: Seduce them, woo them, rule them, protect or "take care" of them.

This perfectly "normal" process of cutting out and killing off what is weak, vulnerable, "feminine"—this is what makes a perfectly ordinary "man." To make a "soldier" is a hyped-up, supercharged process of man making to the tenth power.

I spent five years watching this process of man making among young men—really, babies, in their late teens and early twenties—stationed on nuclear submarines in the U.S. Navy. For five of the years that I was married, my ex-husband and his friends spent days and nights in my apartment, watching movies, drinking, baking chocolate chip cookies, complaining about training and duty, bad-mouthing the worst officers on the boat, drinking some more, telling stories.

M.S. told me he looked forward to "West Pac." A West Pac is a tour of the Western Pacific Ocean, usually for six months or more, when naval crews train, play war games, practice soldiering. The ships dock in Australia, Subic Bay in the Philippines, Hong Kong, Japan—any of the ports in the Western Pacific. M.S. loved West Pac because of the sex. M.S. said, "In the Philippines, every woman is for sale." In the local bars, you could line up against the back wall and get a blow job. You could drink while watching donkeys fuck women. And worse—things I will not write down.

Every person I interviewed who had crossed the equator told me about the initiation ritual in which "pollywogs" (those who have never crossed the equator before) become "shellbacks" (those who have crossed the equator, participated in the ceremony, and received their shellback certificates). This is an elaborate ritual, something in which the entire ship participates. The ritual varies somewhat from group to group, but its basic structure involves pollywogs/initiates crawling through a series of obstacles, reporting to the Royal Court (King

Neptune, the queen, the royal baby) to answer mock charges, and performing tasks assigned by the court. As part of the ritual, the fattest shellback on the ship plays the role of the royal baby: He is stripped down to his underwear; a messy, sticky food (frequently peanut butter) is spread over his stomach; and pollywogs are required to crawl up to his stomach and kiss it (in some variations, they are required to eat a cherry out of his naval). There is also a queen of the court, and, in some versions of this ritual, a paper bag filled with garbage is placed between the "queen's" legs, and the initiate is required to "eat" the "queen's box." Throughout the day, as pollywogs are crawling through the various obstacles designed for them—generally including some version of a tunnel filled with garbage—shellbacks hit them with flexible hoselike objects (sometimes old fire hoses, but frequently objects made with materials available to the crew).

It does not take much analysis to see the relationship between these rituals and the rituals of humiliation and degradation ordinary soldiers used at Abu Ghraib. Pollywogs on their hands and knees, crawling through garbage that quickly accumulated the layers of vomit from those passing through—prisoners, led around on their hands and knees, like dogs, on leashes, smeared with feces. Pollywogs kissing, licking foul matter off a mostly naked fat man's belly—prisoners piled, naked, into pyramids. Pollywogs, putting their heads between the "queen's" legs, into a bag filled with garbage—prisoners, made to masturbate, give oral sex, perform sexual humiliations.

These are the initiation rituals I know about, the life-on-a-boat experiences of the eighteen- to twenty-four-year-old enlisted men who told me their stories. I do not know what the initiation rituals for the army are, what kind of hazing ceremonies the military police responsible for "loosening" prisoners up and posing for pictures in Abu Ghraib went through. But I believe they have their parallels. I believe that their experience of what was "normal" shaped the ways they "prepared" prisoners for "interrogation."

The violence we saw in the photographs released from Abu Ghraib was awful. But we make a mistake when we see this violence as exceptional, as an "evil" that is so far removed from ordinary life as to be unimaginable. For many people in the military, this kind of violence is part of the fabric of the every day. The language of this violence begins in boot camp, with the process of "breaking down" a recruit. The rituals of shaving heads, of verbal abuse, the clichéd faggot-pussy-give-it-to-you-up-your-ass-suck-my-dick taunts of the drill sergeant—these practices are common knowledge, as are the beatings meted out to the weaker men in the unit, the ones who need to be "weeded out."

Before a recruit leaves boot camp, he—and, increasingly, she—is trained in degradation, humiliation. They take this training with them, as part of the identity of "soldier."

This training in degradation and humiliation shapes day-to-day actions, as in the case of "oiling." When a new crew member steps out of place, acts uppity, does not give the proper respect to the veteran crew, the men who are the most fed up get together to teach him a lesson. They take him to a secluded place—on submarines, usually to the engine room, which is hot enough to ensure that people who do not have to will not go there and loud enough to ensure that nobody will hear what is going on. Then they throw him facedown on the floor, tie his hands behind his back, and strip his pants down to his ankles. Depending on how much he struggles, they might tie his feet up, duct tape his mouth shut. They take an oil can—the kind used to oil machinery in the engine room, with a long nozzle and high-pressure injection—insert the nozzle in his anus, and inject him with engine oil.

Every single enlisted man that I knew in the five years I spent on navy bases had heard of this practice. Many had witnessed or participated in an "oiling." They joked about it. They said things like:

"He obviously had something stuck up his ass. We were just trying to help him get it out."

"Now things will run smoothly."

Not one person with whom I talked called this rape. When I said, "That's rape," they all said, "No, it's not like that." Most of them—even the ones who felt sorry for the victim—believed that he "deserved" it.

These men were not at war, just practicing for it. And they were not sadists. They were in and out of my apartment with beer and cigarettes, bumming a meal or a ride, bringing pizza and movies, asking for chocolate chip cookies, organizing trips to the beach, a hike up Diamond Head, a place to store their belongings when they were on West Pac. They were kids—excited, scared, confused, full of themselves, thinking they would live forever, that they were invincible, afraid of dying today or tomorrow. We were all kids, bravado covering scared-and-confused. They had the dumb luck of enlisting in the navy in the 1980s, being stationed in Hawaii—not in Kuwait or Iraq in 1991, not in Afghanistan or Iraq in 2001-to-who-knows-when. Short-staffed and overextended, our armed forces are extending duty in combat zones and recalling troops after they have been sent home. If any one of the men I knew had been through the initiation rituals, the hazing practices, the make-a-man-out-of-you (and this is true for women too) military training for Iraq in 2003, could they have been at Abu Ghraib? Committing acts that would shock and outrage the rest of the world?

Enculturation into the military is designed to strip a person of individual identity, to make loyalty to the group, obedience to superiors, and duty the core of identity. In the mid 1980s, I had the opportunity to interview several lifers—men who had made a career out of the navy, whose loyalties, allegiances, identities were linked to their identity as "sailors." As the Executive Officer of a nuclear submarine explains to me:

> Life on a submarine is very demanding; it requires a lot of work. Initially, a lot of work all the time, a lot of effort, continuous effort to what you are doing, attention to detail, what you're doing. It's dangerous—any ship that goes out, that goes under water, you get a nuclear reactor on there, and you have weapons on board, live steam, and you know there's a lot of hazards to a submarine that goes underwater, so you have to do everything very carefully and train a lot, and it's challenging and it's rewarding to be able to do it, continuously work. It's exciting, too, there are times it's very exciting. So I say it's demanding, challenging, rewarding, and exciting. (A.B., executive officer of a naval nuclear submarine, Pearl Harbor, Hawaii, 1985)

For most of the men I interviewed, the excitement of life in the navy included drinking and sex. C.D., chief of the boat on a naval nuclear submarine, recalls his years in the navy:[3]

> I've been having a good time for thirty years. I really enjoy the navy. I became a professional West Pac-er. West Pacs are great. [When you're] single, West Pacs are—I really enjoyed West Pacs. That's what it's all about, because you go out there and do what submarines are meant to do. There's not much liberty. . . . My first West Pacs were Japan and Subic Bay. They were still recovering from the Korean War. The economy was poor— there was, you know, going to be a bar down there, with twenty or thirty girls all waiting to take you home at night, for a minimal amount of money, so that's the way we lived.

---

3 I conducted these interviews as part of an undergraduate oral history project at the University of Hawaii. I interviewed men serving on nuclear submarines and aircraft carriers and, when possible, their wives. About one-third of these interviews were one-on-one, in-depth discussions with people whom I knew as part of my daily life, but more than half of them were one-on-one interviews with people referred to me as interview subjects and with whom I had no previous relationship before the interviews. I also conducted two group interviews—one with submariners at a party and one with their wives in a private home setting. Selecting quotations for this section poses several challenges. In the first place, although all the people I interviewed signed consent forms allowing our conversations to be taped, not all of them agreed to be quoted. In several cases, I was specifically asked to keep certain information confidential. I have respected this wish. In addition, in the group interview settings, the hierarchy of the boat manifested in the discourse. For example, junior members spoke significantly more than the senior ranking member of the group interview, but their speech was subordinated to the authority of the highest ranking person present (the chief of the boat). Junior members joked more, talked over each other, and incited each other's speech, but they also prompted the chief of the boat to tell stories; at the point at which a story line was invoked, the chief took over the narrative, and the rest of the crew listened attentively. Hence, although many men contributed to the discussions that I quote in this section, the authoritative narrative voice, and hence my direct quotes, come from the chief of the boat. The narrative progression of the interviews with the wives was more complicated. In the first place, fewer women gave me permission to quote from their taped interviews. In the second place, they were in general more hesitant to talk. Hence, I am quoting primarily from one woman who gave me permission to quote from her one-on-one interview. I have tried to be careful to choose material from this interview that was thematically represented in the group interview and in the other one-on-one interviews from which I did not have permission to quote.

When I first got to the PI [Philippines], I can't remember if it was '57 or '59, the streets weren't paved, the beer was warm, the young ladies were lovely, just as they are today. It was fun.

Last time in Hong Kong was '77—the Vietnamese war drove all the prices up for R & R. It ain't no fun to go to Japan anymore. Everything's too expensive. It's more expensive than in the States. . . . It's not that much fun to take a young sailor over there anymore, unless he's going to go on a tour. But as far as going out on the town and having a good time, I've noticed that, uh, in my years, everybody used to look forward to going to Japan. Now we got to stop in Japan for an eight-day upkeep. Why do we got to do that? Can't we go someplace else?

I did these interviews for an oral history project in a folklore class at the University of Hawaii. I did them because I wanted to understand who these people were, the people with whom my ex-husband spent most of his waking hours. I did them because I was afraid of what I did not understand. I still have most of these tapes—almost twenty hours of talking to men in the navy, stationed in Pearl Harbor, Hawaii, and the women who married them. Some of these conversations were one on one, at my kitchen table or in the homes of the people I interviewed. Some of them were in a group setting, at a party for the submarine on which my ex-husband was stationed. At this party, men told me their favorite stories—about when they were drunk, which women they picked up, their exploits and triumphs. One story—a funny story, a story at which everybody around the table talking into the tape recorder laughed—was about "Punchy," "sitting up in this hotel room in Hong Kong, about the fourteenth floor, and this cat came in and disturbed Punchy, and he threw the cat out the window—he looked at it as it went on its flight, and it did not land on its feet. It landed on its head, and it did not survive" (C.D.).

All the stories were about what it meant to be a "good" sailor—a "good sailor" is "anybody that can work all day, drink all night, and pick up the young ladies or the old ladies, whatever happens to be handy, and take them home, no problem" (C.D.).

The men told stories about drinking, sex, fights, the time Punchy killed a cat, and they all laughed. The wives told different stories. Their stories, always, were about how to support the work their husbands were doing. L.M. explained it like this:

> What the wife is supposed to be is an extension of [her] husband. A wife is navy property. We are military property. I am supposed to present myself a certain way because I am a chief's wife. A chief's wife is supposed to be able to keep her husband's guys going and her husband's guys' wives going. The chiefs' wives are not supposed to sit there and say, "Well, the C.O. [commanding officer] did it again," or "I'm so mad about this, this, and this." We are supposed to pretend that everything is okay. We're walking around with rose-colored glasses, everything's fine, there's nothing wrong, there's nothing to worry about, and that's all a bunch of bullshit, because I sit here, and I worry a lot.

Part of what they worry about is the job. One of the wives, L.M., described being married to a submariner as living in a world of secrets, a world defined by what cannot be said, but about which one always speculates. The military operates on a need-to-know basis. Her husband, a junior officer on a Los Angeles class submarine, had a secret clearance, and he was not supposed to discuss with her most of what he did in a day's work. But she was not stupid—she knew that her husband was on a fast-attack, a spy submarine, the first boats out in the case of war—boats and crews charged with sneaking up on the "enemy," gathering surveillance. And, if need be, launching a nuclear missile.

In 1985, when I conducted these interviews, the Soviet Union was still the "enemy" against whom U.S. sailors trained for war. The Cold War still shaped the fears and the fantasies of the men and women with whom I talked. L.M.'s interviews make the shape of these Cold War fears chillingly clear:

> L.M.: I worry constantly. What if you guys get spotted? What if you get watched? What if they find out you're there? My husband told me he's qualified on .45s, and I don't like guns.
> Me: But that's just routine qualifications, right?

L.M.: They have handguns and weapons on board in case they
   get caught in Soviet waters and get boarded.

Me: Does your husband worry about that?

L.M.: They play act. J thinks it's great, it's like cops and robbers.

Me: Cops and robbers?

L.M.: Whenever they're deployed and I know that . . . part
   of their deployment is for spying, you know they go spy,
   and . . . it just scares me. Every time they go out and
   they're going to be going near Soviet waters, I get a little
   scared . . . and then you hear about the cute little Soviet
   boats that stay in international waters. I mean like, there's
   the twelve-mile zone, and they stay in international waters,
   but they get pretty much close to the zone that then it's
   into American waters, and I'm sitting there going, "shoot
   the sucker, get 'em!" I don't care, he may be out there in
   international waters, get 'em, shoot 'em. I mean, when
   they're twelve miles off the coast of Oahu, that does not
   give me a very good sense of security, you know? I mean,
   when I was in Kansas, no Russian. . . . Well, sure, there's the
   KGB—KGB is all over the place. My husband would tell
   me, "be careful what you say over the phone, because the
   KGB are here, too," and I'm like, oh jeez.

Me.: Is he serious?

L.M.: Oh yes, totally serious, absolutely.

*Just six years later, my high school students, with barely a
memory of the Cold War bear, had already taken up the new
enemy against whom they could define themselves: the Muslim,
the Arab, the terrorist.*

All the women with whom I spoke lived lives around a secret center that they learned not to question. They learned not to question their
husbands, to assume that their husbands had good reasons—top-secret
reasons, life-and-death reasons, protecting-the-country reasons—for
what they were doing. If they questioned their husbands, they were,
by extension, questioning the military, the government, all the established order and institutions in charge of our "protection."

And, if you question your husband, you can get him in trouble. Get him in trouble for telling you what he's not supposed to tell you. Get him in trouble for being yourself. Again, L.M. made this point crystal-clear:

> The thing is, there's a lot of things that you can't say, because the potential for getting them into trouble is great. Any little thing can be taken wrong. You know, like, my husband gets upset when I complain about Ronald Reagan. He gets upset about the littlest things. We do not discuss Ronald Reagan. He thinks he would get into trouble for cutting down his boss— he's the commander-in-chief.

This fear of actions or words harming a husband's career was pervasive among the women I interviewed. This fear extended into every space, over every action—at the commissary, at the P.X., dropping children off at school. In public, "what you are supposed to do if you see somebody that obviously outranks your husband [is] keep your mouth shut. If you don't like what they're doing, don't say anything, grin and bear it." No matter what. If you offend somebody who outranks your husband, your husband could be punished:

> It's really hard, because I'm a person who says what I feel. But I have to take into consideration my husband's career. This is what my husband has chosen to do. He and I both don't want something stupid to happen to where it's going to throw those twelve years away. He's going to stay in for the twenty, that is his plan. He wants to stay in for twenty, he wants to retire after twenty years, have that nice little pension. That nice little pension is going to go for paying off a house when we settle somewhere. I'm not going to do anything that I know is going to jeopardize that, and my husband won't either.

Secrecy. Fear. A built-in surveillance—never knowing who is watching, who is listening, learning to self-censor words and actions. The last thing—the last, last, last thing—a "good" wife would ever do is jeopardize her husband's career. A "good" wife lets his secrets lie, keeps his secrets for him. Women's roles, always, to support men.

And a "good sailor"? A "good sailor" is "anybody that can work all day, drink all night, and pick up the young ladies or the old ladies, whatever happens to be handy, and take them home, no problem" (C.D.).

This is how we make a "man."

The child born with the chromosomes and the genitalia that culture uses to define "male" is scripted from the moment a penis is detected. The child trained to be a "boy" quickly learns not to cry. He learns not to show fear. To cry, to show fear, earns him ridicule. He will be called a "sissy," a "pussy"—by his father, his brothers, maybe his sisters and his mother. By children at school. To cry or show fear is to lose his status as "boy" and to become the worst possible thing imaginable: a girl. Before he reaches adolescence, the "boy" already knows that "girls" are inferior. To be a "boy" makes him superior, and, to keep the status that "boy" confers upon him, he must cut out everything in him that is soft, tender, fragile, vulnerable. These things are weak, and on the playground he can be beaten up for showing these things. (Frequently, he may be beaten up at home too.) Tender, soft, vulnerable—these are attributes of "girls," and anything that makes him look like a girl makes him less-than.

A boy's first war is against himself, against what is soft and weak in him—his emotion, his vulnerability, his tenderness.

Frank's wars, that he lost over and over and over again, against the fragility, the vulnerability, of his own body. A war that he could never win.

And is it not these impossible wars against the fragility, the vulnerability, of the flesh that are being fought in Abu Ghraib? I must keep asking: Why *these* acts? Why a pornography of torture? This is the kind of question you have to ask if you were born on an army base in Frankfurt, in the former West Germany, to a mother who went to a French convent school and a father who went twice to Korea and again to Vietnam. Who, when he was upset, would cry that he wished he were back in a firefight, "killing gooks." Who called women sluts and tarts. Who had pictures, in the basement, of "Oriental" women being sexually tortured. Who lined the basement in Alaska with traps for capturing animals—traps whose huge metal jaws could slice through the limbs of moose, elk, caribou. Animals caught in these traps bled—slowly, slowly, slowly, torturously, slowly, torturously—not "to death," usually, but suffered and bled until the one who laid the trap came along and, finally, shot them dead.

This desire for the power over life and death, the delusion that one can be, ultimately, in control of the fragile, vulnerable body.

The Abu Ghraib photographs say this to me:

A small, tiny person, afraid of being ripped open.

The delusion of the one who tortures: I have power, I am whole.

I cannot be fucked, you will not fuck with me, you will not fuck me, you are the fucked.

I am powerful, I am the word, you will obey. I am Sovereign, the Sovereign Body. I am God.

The torturer's God-script: not "Let there be light, and there was light," but "Let there be the darkness and humiliation and despair of your agonized body, ripping open, spilling its insides out, baring itself, abjecting itself, before me, your master. Let the torture I inflict on you carry what is abject in me. When I say, 'Fuck yourself,' and you fuck yourself, I am God."

But does this script not always begin with the small, tiny person, afraid of being ripped open? Who is every bit as much the torturer as the tortured?

Carolyn Nordstrom tells a war story that makes us rethink the pornography of the Abu Ghraib torture photographs. This is the story of a young girl, a refugee from the war in Mozambique, who died after being kidnapped by a group of European pornographers who forced her to have sex with a dog. The story goes like this:

A group of European men were making and marketing pornographic films. Their actions came to light when the dog they were forcing one girl to have sex with mauled her. She was unceremoniously dumped at a hospital. The doctors at the hospital were unable to save the child. The hospital staff, and those they called in to witness the atrocity, were outraged. They petitioned the government to treat this as a formal crime; and the government representatives were equally outraged. Yet no reports hit the presses; no formal court proceedings took place. Officials associated with the Embassy who counted the pornographers as countrymen stepped in to quiet the situation. Leverage was effectively applied. The major offenders were quietly escorted out of Mozambique without any reprisal. The crime was hushed. And the networks that existed to produce these films were not exposed to public or judicial scrutiny. It was left intact. This point is an important one: Atrocities such as using war orphans for pornography do not rest on a few men making a few films. They function as part of a large transnational network of production, distribution, exploitation, and financial gain. They represent an international industry, a multinational non-corporation, no matter how illegal it is. (Nordstrom 1996, 20)

Like all the women in Iraq whom we do not see, this girl in Mozambique, this international pornography ring, has everything to do with you and me. They exist, do what they do, because they can count on our denial, our disavowal. And, when we do happen to catch a glimpse of what we do not want to see, they can count on our forgetting. They counted on these things from the people from whom they bought their equipment, the governments that issued their visas, the venture capitalists that financed their project, the flight crews and host of people that got them in and out of a war zone, into refugee camps, children to steal. They counted on these things from the people who rented them rooms to make their films, who sold them the dog, who cooked and cleaned for them, who produced, edited, advertised, packaged, mailed, and distributed their films, who paid the bribes that allowed all this to happen. They relied on this from the authorities who got them out of Mozambique and back to Europe (Nordstrom 1996, 20–23).

But mostly, they relied on a global culture in which women and children are cheap, expendable, easily bought and sold.

They relied on our wars, making more and more refugees, orphans, women and children whom they can use, because nobody will miss them. Surplus human beings, worth less than a cat or a dog.

The real horror of all this is how much a part of the normal order it is. International sex tourism—including for children—grows in direct relation to the collapse of civil and social structures during wars, to the installation of military and peacekeeping troops, to the belief that some people are discardable, not fully human. We make "enemies" for war and bodies to use and then dispose of in the same way: We count; they do not. We project our fears, act out our desires—for oil or power or domination or control or sex, it all begins to blur in the end—on objects that we cease to see as "human."[4]

My question—perhaps the most important question of my life, in my living: How do we become human beings to each other? How do we become fully human to ourselves?

---

4 For information about these issues, see Nordstrom 1996, 2004; Enloe 2002; Global Fund for Women; U.S. Department of State 2007; and UN Security Council 2009.

INTERLUDE V

On the Violence of Nations
in the Violence of Homes

To make war is an inability with grief. . . . Shame and depression
are an inability with grief. Violence is an inability with grief.

MARTIN PRECHTEL, INTERVIEW WITH REID BAER

A man hates his enemy because he hates his own hate. He says
to himself: this fellow, my enemy, has made me capable of hate.
I hate him not because he is my enemy, not because he hates
me, but because he arouses me to hate. (Wiesel 1982, 198)

On the first day of classes in August 2005, Maria was waiting for me
outside the door to my Introduction to Women's and Gender Studies
class. I didn't recognize her. I could tell, by the way she was looking at
me, that she was hoping for something from me—a sign of recognition,
a greeting, something—something that I didn't have and couldn't give
her. I could see her seeing me not recognize her, see the look on her face
change from a cautious hope to disappointment. When I smiled and
said, "Hello?" and "Can I help you?" Maria's "You don't recognize me?"
held equal parts accusation, anger, disappointment, and defiance.

Even when she told me her name, I still couldn't quite place her.
She had to remind me of the class she had had with me—a year and
a half earlier, she had enrolled in this same Introduction to Women's
and Gender Studies course, but she had had to withdraw from school
because her reserve unit deployed to Iraq. She was supposed to graduate that semester, and maybe she could have, because her unit didn't
actually leave for Iraq until May. But she had to report to Fort Stewart

for training in February, and she couldn't leave the base. Eighteen months later, she was back in Statesboro, trying to get back into the classes she had had to drop, to finish her course requirements, and, finally, to graduate.

It was not really possible, though, for Maria to just come back, a year and half later—to find the things she'd dropped and simply pick them up again. Many of the faculty she had had classes with had left the university. All her friends, her classmates, and support group at Georgia Southern were gone. Because she had had to withdraw from school to go to war, she lost her scholarship money. Actually, she lost it twice. Because she didn't finish her spring 2003 classes, financial aid considered her in "default" and wanted her to pay back the money from the semester she went to war. And, because she had withdrawn, she was no longer eligible for the scholarship. During the time she served in Iraq, Maria went from being an honor roll student on an academic scholarship to being considered "delinquent" and in debt.

She was isolated, alone, with the feeling that her life had been taken away from her. And it had been taken—her old life, her old identity, the old ideas she had about who she was and what a future would be. Every bit of that was gone. She came back a different person. And she came back single. When she left, she was married, with an eighteen-month-old daughter. While she was in Iraq, her husband filed for a divorce. She came home to a three-year-old daughter who could barely remember her, still a semester away from her bachelor's degree. Even this breaking-her-life-up-and-open would have been worth it to her, though, if she hadn't felt betrayed by her government. Maria is patriotic, with a strong belief in the value of serving her country. She didn't want to go to Iraq, but, when she was deployed, she believed that she was being sent for a reason. By the time she came back, she didn't believe in the reasons she'd been given. She was disillusioned and bitter.

Maria spent hours in my office that semester, unpacking her helplessness, her rage, trying to find something "sane" in a world that had gone crazy. One day, when she was still going back and forth between financial aid and the registrar's office, trying to come up with the money to pay for the classes she'd had to drop to go to war on top of the classes she had to retake to graduate, she got a parking ticket. She showed up in my office with the ticket in her hand, shaking, her voice barely able to make its way up through the combusting of her body. She closed the door behind her and stood, silently, in front of my desk.

"Maria, what is it? What happened?"

Rapid breathing, the struggle of a body fighting the desire to hit, shriek, break, kick, scream, yell, punch, beat, stomp, kill. No words.

Move slowly. Very, very slowly. Slow everything. Breathe—deep, slow breaths for Maria. Breathe in, slow, five count. Hold, five count. Breathe out, slow, count to five. Ten times. There. See? We can calm a body combusting. It will be all right—this is my office, a college campus, nothing bad will happen here, it will be all right. Take your time. Breathe. Slow. One . . . two . . . three . . . four . . . five. Hold. Five . . . four . . . three . . . two . . . one. . . .

"I got a parking ticket! After all I have done for my country, while I am in the financial aid offices because they took my scholarship away, and all I want to do is pay for my classes and get back in school. I've been running around this goddamned campus all fucking day, and then I get out to my car and I have a parking ticket, a goddamned parking ticket, after everything I've done for my country, and they can't even let me fucking park my fucking car while I'm trying to finish school? It's the last straw, the last goddamned straw!"

"I just want to take my rifle and open up on everybody!"

"They don't have any idea how close I am to just fucking doing it. They don't have any idea."

Maria was among the first of the soldiers sent to Iraq and among the first to come back. She came back to the news that the nuclear weapons threat had been a lie, and she came back knowing that, even if she could manage to register for classes, she could be pulled out again and sent right back to Iraq. She came back to a college campus that might just as well have been another planet—what sense could she make of her classmates, most of her teachers, the registrar, financial-aid workers, the givers-of-parking tickets? And what sense could they make of her? Could they imagine that she was still living in a body written by the adrenalin-rush fight-or-flight response?

Maria was not in "combat"—she wasn't one of the soldiers breaking into people's homes or taking them for questioning, she wasn't assigned to patrol streets or staff checkpoints, she wasn't a military police officer ordered to "loosen prisoners up" at Abu Ghraib. For most of her time in Iraq, she drove a mail truck back and forth between pick-up and drop-off points. But she was, every single day, afraid of being killed. Of her truck being fired on. Of being in the wrong place at the wrong time when a bomb exploded. Even in the first days of the occu-pation, before the buildup of hopelessness and despair and while sec-tarian groups were still in their organizing stages, the roads were not safe—they were not "safe" for anybody, American or Iraqi. Adrenalin and nerves, nerves and adrenalin—these were the things she lived on. It changed her.

It certainly changed her brain structure. Research on army person-nel stationed in Iraq from April 2003 to May 2005 shows that "living for months at a time on adrenaline also affects brain function." Soldiers deployed to Iraq "did significantly worse in tasks that measured spatial memory, verbal memory and their ability to focus than did 307 soldiers who had not been deployed to Iraq." Though—not surprisingly—they "outperformed those who had not been deployed in a test of reaction time," suggesting that "the soldiers' minds had adapted to the danger-ous, snap-judgment conditions of war." Researchers believe that this happens because the "prefrontal brain area involved in organization and complex spatial memory is knocked out temporarily by high levels of adrenaline" (Morgan, quoted in Carey 2006).[1]

Short-term and verbal memory are impaired, reaction time is heightened. What does this mean for families, for children?

The same semester Maria had to withdraw to go to war, one of her classmates, Tammy, was writing letters to her husband in Kuwait. He was in one of the first army units to deploy in preparation for the March invasion. While Maria's reserve unit was training at Fort Stewart, Tammy's husband was already in the Middle East. In all our conversations, Tammy described her husband as a man who was gen-tle, kind, and compassionate. Part of an extended family, a favorite son of a mother who doted on him, Tammy's biggest domestic problem was keeping her husband from giving too much. Anything a family member needed—brother, sister, mother, father, fourth cousin of an

---

1 For a summary of this study, see Carey 2008. For a more scientific analysis of the study, see Vasterling et al. 2006.

in-law—he was there with it. Tammy wanted to keep a few more things for her immediate family and was sometimes frustrated by her husband's too-generous nature. But that generosity of spirit was also what she loved about him, and she told the stories of her frustrated attempts to accumulate capital and possessions with a humor and indulgence that left her classmates laughing with her, at the image of this kindly give-everything-away husband.

When her husband got back from Iraq, Tammy's problems were different. She came to my office one day, shut the door, and asked if she could just sit down a minute. She said she just didn't know what to do, who to talk to. She and her husband were fighting.

"He gets mad about the least little thing. He's never been like this before."

"He yells at me, and I try to understand, try to remember that he's been through things, but sometimes I can't help it, and I cry."

Crying triggered him even more, made him angrier and more out of control. Sometimes, when Tammy cried, her husband hit her.

Tammy and Maria were among the first students at my university who brought into the open the problems of living after Iraq. For Maria, I scheduled an appointment with the dean of students, with whom we discussed some of the most urgent needs of students who had been to Iraq and were coming back to school—things like working out withdrawals without academic penalty, the problems with scholarship money and registration. For Tammy, who had already graduated, there wasn't much I could do. She was no longer eligible for counseling sessions through our health services program, and the best I could do was to direct her to family services at Fort Stewart. But she was afraid of contacting family services—that would be like "telling on" her husband, it might get him in trouble.

Our university did work out the financial problems for Maria, did get her registered and back in school. But none of us were any help to Maria or to Tammy's husband with their biggest problems—their frustration, rage, fear, helplessness, their difficulty adjusting to "normal" life after Iraq. Even as I write these lines, we are still failing them. Maria, Tammy, their families—they are all living the after-life of war, an after-life that brings violence into living rooms and bedrooms, turns the kitchen table into a battle zone.

W ar lives in our homes in other, darker ways. Dave Grossman, an army psychologist who has spent his career helping combat veterans, writes about the sexual pleasure men can find in killing:

> The linkage between sex and killing becomes unpleasantly apparent when we enter the realm of warfare. Many societies have long recognized the existence of this twisted region in which battle, like sex, is a milestone in adolescent masculinity. Yet the sexual aspects of killing continue beyond the region in which both are thought to be rites of manhood and into the area in which killing becomes like sex and sex like killing. (Grossman 1995, 136)

One of the men he worked with told him:

> Squeezing the trigger—releasing a hail of bullets—gives enormous pleasure and satisfaction. These are the pleasures of combat, not in terms of the intellectual planning—of the tactical and strategic chess game—but of the primal aggression, the release, and the orgasmic discharge. (Shalit, quoted in Grossman 1995, 136)

Grossman writes:

> A gun is power. To some people carrying a gun is like having a hard-on. It was a pure sexual trip every time you got to pull the trigger. Many men who have carried and fired a gun—especially a fully automatic weapon—must confess in their hearts that the power and pleasure of explosively spewing a stream of bullets is akin to the emotions felt when explosively spewing a stream of semen. (1995, 136)
>
> The concept of sex as a process of domination and defeat is closely related to the lust for rape and the trauma associated with the rape victim. Thrusting the sexual appendage (the penis) deep into the body of the victim can be perversely linked

to thrusting the killing appendage (a bayonet or knife) deep into the body of the victim.

This process can be seen in pornographic movies in which the sexual act is twisted, such that the male ejaculates—or "shoots his wad"—into a female's face. The grip of a firer on the pistol grip of a gun is much like the grip on an erect penis, and holding the penis in this fashion while ejaculating into the victim's face is at some level an action of domination and symbolic of destruction. The culmination of this intertwining of sex and death can be seen in snuff films, in which a victim is raped and then murdered on film. (1995, 137)

A viewfinder in the basement of Alaska. Abu Ghraib. Tammy's bedroom.

These men who grow to love killing like orgasm come home to lovers, families, children. What does "intimacy" mean after this? When they make love, what fantasies play out in their heads?

The violence of war lives on and on in the psyches, the fantasies, the families of the soldier. Dubravka Zarkov, a social scientist at the Institute of Social Studies in the Netherlands, has studied the role of sexual violence in the wars devastating the Balkans throughout the 1990s. She tells us that "war can surely never be said to start and end at a clearly defined moment. Rather, it seems part of a continuum of conflict" (Zarkov and Cockburn 2002, 10) When we can see that "war" is something that builds from violences that exist before "war" is ever declared and continues to evolve as violences long after it has supposedly "ended," then we can understand that war is part of a "continuum of violence" that "runs through the social sphere, and the economic and political spheres" (Zarkov and Cockburn 2002, 10). Understanding this continuum of violence allows us to see, clearly, that the "prevalence of male sexualized violence against women and children, in both war and peace," is on this continuum (10).

When I make this point to students in my Women's and Gender Studies classes, they are, at first, shocked. Disbelieving. I am equally stunned that they do not see what to me seems so obvious. Even when we read such books as Grossman's and the students begin to see the evidence of this continuum of violence, they do not see that our entire society is militarized. I see evidence of this militarization everywhere—in the ROTC programs on our college campuses, the shooting range that sits right behind the ceramics studio at Georgia Southern. In the army, navy, air force, and marine recruiters that line the halls of our high schools. In the fact that our military has a budget of almost $550 billion, plus an additional $170 billion for the wars in Iraq and Afghanistan—larger than almost all the rest of the world's military expenditures combined. In the commercials advertising "Be all you can be" and "The few, the proud, the marines." In the camouflage designs on children's t-shirts, pajamas, shorts, and slacks. In the games our children play—*Full Spectrum Warrior, SOCOM II: Navy Seals, Halo 3, BioShock, Gears of War, Assassin's Creed, Dead Rising, Call of Duty, F.E.A.R. First Encounter Assault Recon*—the list goes on.

But mostly, I see this militarization in the ways that we perform the roles of "man" and "woman." Militarization makes us think that it is "normal" to tear the tenderness out of little boys, to beat the crying out of them and turn them into "men" who never learn the words for their own emotions. Militarization makes us think it is normal to send teenagers to war, to teach them to drink themselves numb to drown their natural fears, and to let rage, lust, and violence take them over. Militarization makes us believe that men's violence is "natural." It blinds us to the lifelong labor required to cut out all that is "soft," "weak," and "feminine" and make some men learn to love to kill. Militarization makes us idealize a hypermasculinized caricature of a human being and to scorn the many men—most men, in my experience—who struggle against their own softness, their fear, the tenderness they can express only with women.

We are surrounded by men who disprove the lie that militarized masculinity is "normal." But, instead of recognizing in them the hope and possibility of a future beyond the wars we make, we call them names—pussy, faggot. We pretend that *they* are the aberration, "abnormal" and "failed." But look around you. Who really embodies this hypermasculine ideal? It is not "normal."

Militarized hypermasculinity twists and deforms women too. The more a culture idealizes "hard," "strong," and "aggressive" men, the more it fetishizes "femininity" in women. Where men train bodies to be big, hard, strong, women starve bodies to be thin—firm, yes, but also "soft" and "round": breasts, buttocks, and vaginas are the quintessential fantasized "feminine." We know that women extensively damage their own bodies by wearing crippling high heels. The damage they do to their bodies goes far beyond the familiar bunions, hammer toes, sprained ankles, and backs thrown out. Prolonged use of high heels shrinks the Achilles tendon and causes premature osteoarthritis in the knees as well as nerve damage in the feet. But women wear high heels anyway—the trademark of the pornographic centerfold, acting out a male sexual fantasy that is destructive to their own bodies.

The high heel as sexual fetish has its counterpart in the practice of foot binding.

The bound foot—besides crippling women, besides ensuring that their bodies could always be controlled by men—was a sexual fetish.

The high heel. The bound foot. A viewfinder in the basement of Alaska. Abu Ghraib.

Even when we see these relationships, most women cannot let go of their high heels. Trained to feel that "value" comes from being sexually desirable, we cling to the source of our own disfigurement to feel "sexy." "Attractive." What revolution in consciousness would it take to see what is ugly in this fetish?

We can connect the dots between the high heel and the kind of "man" who comes to feel that "carrying a gun is like having a hard-on," where "the power and pleasure of explosively spewing a stream of bullets" is like "explosively spewing a stream of semen" . . . a "pure sexual trip every time you got to pull the trigger" (Grossman 1995, 136).

The cum shot. Abu Ghraib.

Some Dots to Connect

Researchers looking at patterns of torture in South America have found that all existing reports about torture indicate that the female body was always a "special" object for torturers. The treatment of women always included a high degree of sexual violence. Women's bodies—their vagina, uterus, and breasts— linked to women's identities as sexual objects, as wives and mothers, were clear objects of sexual torture. (Bunster 1991 and Taylor 1997, quoted in Jelin 2003, 79)

Sexual violence is a part of men's torture too—but, for men, it is a matter of turning them into women, of a "feminization" in which they were "transformed into passive, impotent, and dependent beings" (Jelin 2003, 79). And torture, always, established the "virility" of the military—the power of the military "man."

This continuum of violence is screaming for us to recognize it, interrupt it, change it. When we really look, it is easy to see how the violences in our homes are the logical continuation of the social order that shapes our notions of gender, of family, and of nation. Veena Das, an anthropologist who has studied the institutional processes through which violence and suffering are produced, argues that this violence is embedded in the social contract. The social contract is always also a sexual contract that "places the reproductive capacities of women within male-dominated family" structures (2007, 26). Women give up their last names and take on their husbands.' Sons are still more valued than daughters—they carry on the family name of the father (not of the mother). And, of course, it is the job of the good mother to raise sons who can fight her country's wars. Most of the world's religions still see women as subordinate, see men as closer to God and the heads of the household.

Religion, family, nation—all conspire to preserve a social order that gives men dominance over women.

These things are obvious. And, obviously, where women are considered inferior, dependent, kept from economic and political power, they are subject to the violence of men—a violence that, as we have seen, inhabits every aspect of domestic and public life, from living rooms and kitchens and bedrooms to work places, city streets, the world-turned-war-zone. But what might not be so obvious is that sexual desire is invested in the nation itself—that "nation-making appropriates women's bodies as objects on which the desire for nationalism [can] be brutally inscribed and a memory of the future made" (Das 2007, 38).

Sexual desire inscribed in the nation? Nation making as an appropriation of women's bodies as objects?

Consider this: Patrick Cammaert, former UN force commander in the Congo, says that it is "more dangerous to be a woman than to be a soldier" (Kristof 2008). In the Congo, up to three-quarters of the women in several areas have been raped. In Darfur, rape victims are typically scarred or branded to advertise that they have been raped, conquered, that an opposing militia has taken over this body-as-territory. This mutilation "is often done by police officers or soldiers, in uniform, as part of a coordinated government policy" (Kristof 2008). Similarly, during the Balkan wars in the 1990s, the organized, brutal, and systematic rape of Bosnian and Muslim women was part of a strategy of "ethnic cleansing."

Over and over again, we see rape as a systematic tactic of war by which militaries terrorize civilian populations, assert their dominance and control, and, in many cases, intentionally impregnate women. Under social systems in which women are subordinated to men—as wives, mothers, bearers of the name of the father—to impregnate a woman is to break up home and family, to literally take from the enemy the emblem of his masculinity—his wife, his daughters, his home, his honor. To rape and impregnate the wives, daughters, mothers of the "enemy" is to take possession of the future of the nation, a future that is, literally, written in blood—the blood of raped women, the blood of the soldier rapist that turns women into breeders for the opposing military.

How much more literal can this be? To impose a "nation" is to take possession of the reproductive capacities of women, to take their bodies as sexual objects and make them carry the children of the men who conquer them.

This is how sexual desire is inscribed in the nation, how nation making is an appropriation of women's bodies as objects.

Veena Das calls this social order criminal (2007, 61). I agree with her.

It is criminal, but it is not inevitable. Nationalism, militarism, and patriarchy are not inevitable. Everywhere, all around us, we see individuals, organizations, institutions, religions, movements that show us other possibilities. The Quakers. Men Stopping Violence. The Women's International League for Peace and Freedom. Mouths Wide Open: The Army Men Project. Women in Black. Veterans for Peace. Iraq Veterans Against the War. Coalition for Peace and Action. Grandmothers for Peace. The Dalai Lama. Thich Nhat Hanh. The power of the Buddhist traditions. Parents, Families, and Friends of Lesbians and Gays. The International Foundation for Gender Education. Gender DynamiX. Human Rights Watch.

Hundreds more exist—hundreds and hundreds, without even looking far. So what kind of self-destructive insanity is it to cling to our violent structures of gender, nation, and military as though these are inevitable when we are surrounded by overwhelming evidence of possibilities for being otherwise?

They are not inevitable. We have made these systems up. In fact, Michael Kaufman argues that "the various forms of violence against women" are an "expression of the fragility of masculinity" (2007, 44). "Masculinity is terrifyingly fragile because it does not really exist . . . as a biological reality. It exists as ideology; it exists as scripted behavior; it exists within gendered relationships" (42). It exists as a fantasy, always about to be exposed as illusion, sleight of hand, a huge, violent, destructive sham. If we see that masculinity is an ideology, not a biological reality, then we can see that the violence of our social order is "many things at once. At the same instant, it is the individual man acting out relations of sexual power; it is the violence of a society—a hierarchical, authoritarian, sexist, class-divided, militarist, racist, impersonal, crazy society—being focused through an individual man onto an individual woman" (33).

If we believe that the violences structuring our social order are not inevitable—as I do—then the questions for us to ask are these: How is violence (histories of violence) embedded into different patterns of sociality? (Das 2007, 103). How can our strategies for demilitarization and peace "include a strategy of change in masculinities?" (Connell 2007, 38). To evolve—I would say to survive—we have to first rescript "masculinity" and rewrite our entire, failed, doomed system of heterosexist gender relations. We have to change the ways that we think of ourselves as "men" and "women."

This seems to me so clear, so simple, so obvious. I know that, when I say this, many people feel it as a direct threat, an attack on the structure of their identities. If we have mastered a gender role and are "good" at it—that is, we get our sense of value, power, and identity from it—how could we want to abandon it? If our religions say "men" are this and "women" are that, and we buy into it—how could we want to go against that? But, every single day, women live the direct threat of the violence of our ideologies of gender. So how do we weigh the difference between those threats? On the one hand, the psychological threat that says, "We have to change our identities because our ideas about what 'man' and 'woman' are create violence in the world." On the other hand, the beatings, rapes, murders, wars that our old ideas of "man" and "woman" make. So which weighs more?

The scale: Katherine MacKinnon points out that when the Twin Towers of the World Trade Center were attacked on September 11, 2001, between 2,800 and 3,000 people were killed in this act of terrorism. The United States launched a "war on terror" as retaliation. Every year in the United States, this same number of women are murdered by men. We do not call this terrorism. We have not gone to war against the "terrorist threat" of our gender relations—gender relations in which a woman is raped every four minutes, in which women are murdered by their husbands, boyfriends, lovers, in which women are bought and sold for sex, in which the Centers for Disease Control and Prevention calls family violence a "national epidemic." We do not call this terrorism—we call it normal and put tiny bandages on wounds gushing blood. On our college campuses, we respond to the real danger women are in by giving them rides across campus at night. We distribute whistles and tell them not to walk alone after dark, not to let other people buy them drinks. We ignore the insanity of a social order in which the sexual danger we warn them about is considered "normal."[2]

So what counts as "terrorism"? How do we call the pervasive, sustained violence structuring and structured by our systems of gender "normal"? The common denominator running through the social order—family, state, nation, military, economy, government, church— is a gender system (coupled with systems of class and race) that produces violence. And it is not "natural"—we have made it up.

Again, my question: Can we make up something different?

---

2   For more information about these issues, see MacKinnon 2006 and Dorner and Graff 1989.

11

TOWARD RE-MEMBERING
A FUTURE

If we are to get out of destructive cycles of war and violence, we have to change our mental representations of our SELVES as well as of others. (Volkan 1988, 76)

There can be no such thing as "peace" unless we change our gender relations. (Connell 2007, 38)

If we want to choose a future of life, love, and hope, we have to change the way we think. About who is "us" and who is "them," about who "we" are and who the "other" is. About what it means to be a "man" or a "woman." We have to rethink all our old binaries. Our divisions of the world—into man/woman, good/evil, black/white, inside/outside, enemy/ally—have us trapped in roles that are killing us.

Killing us like this:

As of 2006, thirty-two countries were actively engaged in armed conflict (Buhaug et al. 2007), and "an estimated 300,000 child soldiers—boys and girls under the age of 18—are involved in more than 30 conflicts worldwide" (UNICEF 2007). The United States, which is the largest supplier of arms to developing nations, accounts for half the entire world's trade in arms and military expenditures—a world trade that has topped $1 trillion (Shah 2009). These wars ravage families and countries, contributing to the dire poverty afflicting so many people. War and poverty make refugees and slaves. The Office of the UN High Commissioner for Refugees (UNHCR) reports that, after several years of decline, "the global number of people affected by conflict-induced internal displacement increased from 24.4 to 26 million" by the end of 2007. Refugees and slaves. Today, more than twenty-seven million people are forced into slavery in every country in the world, including the United States. In fact, "human trafficking is the third most lucrative criminal activity in the world after illegal drugs and black-market guns, generating $9.5 billion in annual revenue" (Global Fund for Women [GFW]).

Women and children are especially vulnerable to the economic and cultural devastation that war brings. "Women constitute 70 percent of the world's 1.3 billion absolute poor, those living on less than $1/day" (GFW). How can we be surprised that at the core of their vulnerability is their sexual bodies, when, "to some people, carrying a gun is like having a hard on" (Grossman 1995, 136)? Researchers studying women's lives in war and postwar societies have shown us that any largely male force—an army, the U.N. "peacekeeping" troops, humanitarian and international aid organizations, police forces—increase the demand for prostitution. "The arrival of soldiers is often associated with a sudden rise in child prostitution and sex tourism, and an expansion of sex trafficking in the region" (GFW).

And traffickers prey upon refugees. A 2006 UNHCR study finds that "abductions or kidnapping (especially of girls and women); trafficking of women and girls; forced prostitution; and disappearances of women and girls" were common among refugee populations (da Costa 2006, 16). Women and children who do not count—refugees, the starving poor in countries ravaged by war, the too-many children that families cannot feed—are cheap. We buy them, sell them, keep them as slaves. For sex, for agricultural and domestic work, in our factories. We use them up and throw them away.[1]

This is a nightmare. My question, the same question, over and over again: Can we wake up from our collective violences? Can we dream our alternatives into being?

[1] For more information about these issues, in addition to the Global Fund for Women and U.S. Department of State 2007, see Buhaug et al. 2007; Hellman and Sharp 2008; and Shah 2009.

Re-membering as Mourning:
A Possibility for Waking

In 1986, I went to Germany with my ex-husband and his family for his brother's wedding. This was a disastrous trip, made in my nightmare days, when I almost let myself not have to live anymore.

One day, Lewis and I were at his brother's apartment, watching television in the living room while his brother looked over wedding pictures with his new wife and the photographer. I don't remember what we were watching, but whatever it was included a rape scene. I have the memory of a brutal rape, a horrid, horrid scene. I was so young, so stupid, carrying open wounds from a life I had not even begun to be able to look at—I didn't have enough understanding then or the language with which to say, "This is why this representation is part of the violence I must stand against." I just cried. I couldn't help it—the scene triggered me so badly, I just started crying, and I couldn't stop. My crying triggered Lewis. He thought his brother would think he was doing something bad to me. He told me to shut up, angrily, and that just made me cry harder. He snapped; he grabbed me by the shoulders and shoved my head into the back of the sofa to muffle the sounds of my crying. I couldn't breathe. I struggled to get away, and the more I struggled, the angrier he got. I finally broke free, but he came toward me. I was terrified, and, without thinking, reflex-response, I swung my right arm forward, fist balled up; when he got close to me, I punched him. Just punched him—in the nose, just punched him.

I think, at that moment, he really wanted to kill me. I saw him hold himself back, like his whole body could snap and snap me with it. He didn't hit me again, though. But he did worse. He told me I should be raped, somebody should shove a broom handle up my ass—more things than that, but I don't remember the rest. His voice had so much hate in it, the things he was saying and the voice he was using were worse than any hitting-kicking-punching he could have done to me. Still, when his brother—who had heard cries, sounds of violence—came back to see what was wrong, we both said nothing.

Now, here's the thing. I stayed in that apartment, with Lewis. I pretended that everything was fine. (But who could have believed that? I was constantly red-eyed from crying.) I stayed there, with Lewis and his family, with his brother's wife and her family. I went sightseeing with all of them, made small talk, did social things. A few days before we left, the bride's and groom's families had dinner at the Stuttgart TV tower. Before dinner, we went up the tower to the observation deck, where we spent some time admiring Stuttgart's skyline. On the top of that tower, looking down at the city, I was filled with such a strong desire to let the force of gravity take me over. It seemed like too much work to keep holding myself upright. I was so close to letting myself fall—not "jumping" so much as simply relaxing all my muscles and letting myself glide the 712 feet to a ground that would have freed me from the burden of living any longer. I've had to make my way through can't-live-in-this-world-any-more thoughts before, but this was the closest I've come to giving in to the force of them. Lewis's brother saw me, though. He came over to the rail I was leaning on, real quiet and calmlike, and he looked at me dead on and said, "You'd better not. Don't even think about it anymore."

I don't know what would have happened if Chris hadn't come. I want to think I would have found the energy to pull myself up. I remember thinking that, if I let myself fall, I would be doing violence to the people there. The witnesses would be traumatized. Then there would be all the work that death means. A body to transport, forms to fill out. I couldn't imagine how many forms it would take to get a body from the bottom of the Stuttgart TV tower back to the United States. And it would ruin Chris's wedding. This worry about traumatizing people and ruining Chris's wedding was a force up, working against the force of the gravity pulling at my body. My force up and Chris coming pulled me away from the rail, in to dinner, and through the remaining days until our scheduled departure from Germany. When I left, it was with Lewis and his family—Lewis still not talking to me, the force of gravity still calling to me.

It was six years after almost letting myself fall before I realized that, all along, I had had another "choice." It was after I found Kathrin and was undertaking this work of re-membering, which is also a mourning, that I could re-member this scene with a different ending. I remembered everything, right up to the moment that I broke free of Lewis's grip holding my face in the sofa. Then I imagined myself, very calmly, collecting my purse and my plane ticket, walking out the front door, hailing a taxi, going to the airport, and getting myself on standby for the first plane back to the States. It wouldn't have been hard. I could've done it. It wouldn't have cost much. *I could have done that!*

But, at the time, I didn't *know* I could do that. None of these things ever occurred to me. So did I really have the "choice"?

Now, I would never be in that situation in the first place. But this is now, not then. And, if that was me then, what, really, is the difference between me and my mother? Between me and Jenny?

The question for me, then, is this: How do we begin to see other options, other possibilities? How do we shift our feeling, our thinking, our vision? From inside my hurt, pain, shame, rage, what "choices" did I really have? From that place, I could not find hope or strength, compassion or love. How do we "choose" these when they are not visible to us? If somebody opens a path to me, shows me where to get the tools I need and how to use them, and I turn down both path and tools, then, yes, I can say I have made a choice. But if I see neither path nor tools, how can I be said to be choosing against them?

A Possible Path

Veena Das asks, "What is it to bear witness to the criminality of the social rule—to inhabit the world, or inhabit it again, in a gesture of mourning?" (2007, 62). If you have lived through the refugee camp— or the concentration camp, or the rape-as-a-tactic-of-war zone, or the steady bombing of your life and world in Iraq, or being kidnapped and tortured by the military juntas in South America, the apartheid government in South Africa, the war-on-terror government of the United States (the list goes on and on)—if you have lived through these things, how do you emerge from them and try, after all that you have seen, to make up a "normal" life? To find a job, buy a house, shop for groceries, meet your lover for dinner at six every evening? How do you wake up every morning and believe in the possibility of going on? When you know what humans are capable of doing? When every act of kindness, love, generosity, compassion is always already shadowed by the brutal violence you have experienced?

This knowledge of what humans are capable of is what Das calls "poisonous knowledge." Poisonous knowledge is always present. Unlike traumatic memories, which may lurk in an unconscious, tucked away until a trigger evokes them or sleep lets them seep into dreams, poisonous knowledge is present in every word, every gesture, every touch. It shapes what we do and do not speak, who we do and do not trust, how we raise our children, dress, walk, talk. It directs if, when, how we make love. Pain is the "acknowledgement and recognition" of this poisonous knowledge (Das 2007, 57).

Some ways of living with and remembering pain feed it, grow it, make it fuel hate and rage. Mourning, though, can lead us through our pain and to compassion, love, hope. Mourning acknowledges pain, grief, the presence of violence, and, *by acknowledging* it, creates "a home for the mutilated and violated self of the other" (Das 2007, 47–48). To make *through our mourning* a home for the other is to bear witness to the criminality of the social order, but it is also to bear witness to the forces of love and life in our relations. The kind word. The look of understanding. The one who bears our tears without flinching. The one who feels our pain and returns it with a gesture of compassion.

To bear witness through the gesture of mourning is to establish a knowing relationship with death. With death as immanent, to our bodies as fragile things that are easily hurt, mutilated, tortured, killed. But the mourning that allows us to live in a healing way with the knowledge of death and violence requires its own way of remembering. Tzvetan Todorov calls the kind of memory that can help mourning and healing "exemplary" and the kind of memory that keeps us stuck in pain and suffering "literal." Literal memory is self-referential. In this way of remembering, we rehearse, over and over, the litany of wrongs done to us. We are the innocent victims who suffer, whose suffering nobody else can imagine, and we suffer from the actions of a guilty perpetrator, the evil other. Literal memory is static, stuck, and its repetition of this history of suffering reentrenches pain, anger, hatred (Todorov 1997, 20). In contrast, exemplary memory connects us to the suffering of others and to the world around us. In this way of remembering, we see that all events have a history, a context, a trajectory into the future. We see human actors as being like us (Todorov 1997, 20).

If, for example, we remember the experience of being raped in an exemplary way, we remember that, in the United States, one in four women and one in ten men will be hurt by sexual violence. We remember that rape is a strategy for exerting power and control. That it is encouraged in prisons as a tactic for subduing inmates. That it is a fundamental part of any war. In this way of remembering, we see that what we suffer is not unique—it is part of a pattern in a social fabric that needs to be remade. Exemplary memory looks for and works at the knots of the social fabric as it loosens the knots of our own pain. It is thus a way of engaging in social action. It is a way of remembering that brings the past into the present in order to affirm life over death, love over hate, hope over despair, compassion over violence. It is a force up, a way to stand up against the gravity calling to our weary bodies, a way to stand still against the pain yelling through our raging bodies. It is a way of living with poisonous knowledge without in turn poisoning the world around us.

This re-membering is also a grieving. Re-membering the Germany scene with Kathrin, I could picture Lewis as a man in pain—struggling, confused, scared, raging against his own demons. Lewis, at ten years old, left home alone to care for his younger brother and sister while his divorced mother worked the night shift at the local Kraft plant. When I cried—to him, inexplicably—at a rape scene that triggered me, what did I trigger in Lewis? Who, at ten years old, could spin out of control by fear, guilt, and anger when his brother cried and he didn't know why, didn't know what to do to comfort a four-year-old and make the crying stop. I could imagine other things that lived in this fear: his father, telling him he was bringing him and his sister to their grandparents to visit when, in fact, he was leaving them there for good. Children in excess, wanted by neither parent. His guilt, his shame, his fear, his rage, and my crying a trigger that snapped him.

Re-membering as mourning allowed me to connect Lewis's pain to my own, to see both of us as wounded children acting out our old emotion. Mourning allows us to move past a world of pure villains and innocent victims. It allows us to see the complexity of our emotion, our actions. Re-membering as mourning allows us to see the underside of violence: old wounds, old pain, histories crying for the compassion they never received.

But it does not demand that we sacrifice ourselves to the violence unleashed on us. Rather, mourning can allow us to let go. Mourning showed me that, in Germany, I had an option—to pick up my purse, walk out the door, call a cab, and fly standby back to the United

States. Most important, mourning allowed me to forgive myself for not being able to see, at twenty-three, that that option was available to me. Mourning gives us our compassion—for ourselves as much as for others.

Frank never mourned. Instead, he rehearsed, over and over again, his past suffering, his injuries, his grief. For Frank, "remembering" was a death work that endlessly repeated the litany of wrongs done to him and so dug him deeper and deeper into his pain. Remembering grew his hatred and his rage. I do not want this kind of remembering. Remembering for a future is a creative act. It is a way of remapping shattered psyches, fractured bodies. It is an archeological project that rehinges the bones of our haunting ghosts so they can find their peace. Our remembering is a birthing, a labor that generates and transforms the social world (Jelin 2003, 5). It is our possibility for becoming fully human to ourselves, for seeing our "others" as human, like us.

The Work of Re-membering

I can be overwhelmed, simply overwhelmed, by the enormity of the violences in this world. The struggles of my own life are nothing next to the pain and suffering that so many endure. If I had had to live through having my life destroyed, my home bombed, the people I love tortured, maimed, killed, my land taken, my rivers polluted, my economy and government ruined, my future made hopeless—if I had had to live through any of this, how could I ever have found a way past the rage that is fed, every single day, by these atrocities? How could I have begun to imagine how to cultivate my compassion, to reach for the love that can re-member the futures we have to make?

Primo Levi, in *The Drowned and the Saved,* writes that, after Auschwitz, anybody who believes God exists is a fool. Part of me agrees with him. And we do not have to go to the extreme case of Auschwitz or to the rape camps in Bosnia or to the genocides in Rwanda or Darfur to see this. I see, every semester, another handful of students writhing in the pain their lives have made. M, whose father raped her when she was an infant, broke her bones, raped her more. L, who told me, one night in my office, that she could not get help for the strain in her neck, because she might have to reveal the cuts on her shoulders. She used a razor blade to slice her skin—under her shirt, where nobody would notice—because it brought the pain diffused through her body into a sharp, clear focus. Or the three women in my Sex, Violence, and Culture class, the first semester I taught it, whose mothers and aunts were killed by their male partners. The list goes on and on. Every semester, I have at least five students whose lives have been shaped by violence.

And then there is Z. After a semester of not being able to do his work, coming to class high, fucked up, he told me:

"I have a sadistic personality."

"I think I am a sociopath—I fit the description of a sociopath—but my shrink doesn't think I am. But he does think I have a sadistic personality disorder."

"The only reason I don't do the things I think about doing is because I could get in trouble. It is self-preservation. I don't want to go to jail."

I believe he was serious.

For these students, what does "pleasure" mean? Joy? Hope? Love? What could it mean for them to remember for a future?

If Frank had not left, if I had had to live the last twenty years in fear of Frank, carrying his secrets, could I ever have found my way through the raging pain that was eating me? Under the constant weight of his presence, could the grip the death drive had on me ever have loosened enough to allow me to take up the work of love?

It *is* possible. Even under the most horrific conditions, among the least likely people, we see love working—like in Angola, where a group of children turned storm drains under a city street into a home. Nordstrom writes of her visit with them:

> In this drain the children had created a home and a community. It was spotlessly clean. I remember being surprised that there was no smell. The children had lined the walls with pictures from magazines, no small feat for children with no money for food and clothing, much less glue. An old inner tube from a tire served as a chair. The children had somehow acquired scraps of fabric and rug and placed them on top of cardboard, lining the floors in home-style comfort. . . . The children sat

me down next to an old powdered milk tin can connected to a strange assembly of wires and small bits of transistor boards connected by yet more wires. Delightedly, they turned on the radio. They had even fashioned a dial so they could tune in different stations. . . . With a lump in my throat, I asked the children who had made this. They pointed to a boy of about eight, who grinned in recognition.

This is a community in the fullest sense. The children have instituted a strong code of conduct. They share everything they have with each other equally. Stealing isn't allowed, and if someone does steal, the children have a governing council where everyone sits down and finds a solution. They assign chores. . . . [T]hey even instituted a security system for protection. If one is taken by the police, all the others go to find odd jobs like washing cars or shining shoes, or maybe stealing, to scrape together the money to take to the jail and get their friend out. . . . In a world of violence, they have sought to create stability and accord. As one youth told me, "I carry a little bit of peace in my heart wherever I go, and I take it out at night and look at it." (2004, 176–177)

Next to these children, I am humbled. From the inside of war, in the midst of the death work surrounding them, they live the work of life and love and hope. To re-member a future is to remember these children.

It is precisely because the death drive has such force, precisely because we are killing and dying from the ways we rehearse, over and over again, our old wounds, our hatreds, that I have to find the energy, the voice, the courage to stand up and join in the work so many others are already doing: a work of love that affirms life against the force of this death drive. We can call our violences "human nature" and declare that war has always been and will always be, because we forget that these children in Angola are also part of our "nature" as humans. To believe that greed or men's testosterone or a distorted version of "survival of the fittest" prevents us from evolving beyond our violence erases these children, forgets the millions of children like them. It forgets the millions of people, women and men, from every time and place in the world, who show us the possibility of love, compassion, the part of our nature that chooses the work of love and life over the work of hatred and death.

This, too, is "human nature": Women's International League for Peace and Freedom, the Peace Factory Cyberworks, Grandmothers for Peace International, Search for Common Ground, Global Fund for Women, Women to Women International, International Peace Bureau, Pathways to Peace, National Peace Foundation, Anti-War.com, United for Peace, Code Pink, Fellowship of Reconciliation, True Majority, Peace Boat, Women in Black, Global Action to Prevent War, Global Peace Initiative, World without War Council, Veterans for Peace, Baring Witness.

As I said before, hundreds of these kinds of organizations exist and include millions of members. They are everywhere, all around us, if we choose to look. They are my force up.

But this force up cannot lift us without a change in the gender order. Dubravka Zarkov and Cynthia Cockburn argue that "a transformation of the gender order" is the underpinning of peace and a "necessary component of any lasting peace process" (2002, 11). I agree with them. We cannot see the possibilities for being otherwise that these Angolan children and hundreds of peace organizations show us as long as we see, always, "man" as "soldier" and "woman" as man's "other"— his opposite, the one thing that a "real" man would never, ever, ever be. Weak. Emotional. Soft. A pussy.

Object relations theory gives us a way to trace this splitting-off of the self back to infancy. In *The Need to Have Enemies and Allies*, Vamik Volkan explains that the infant knows, first and foremost, "good" and "bad" feeling states—the body as warm, safe, secure, hungry, thirsty, cold, wet. And it knows its first objects in relation to these "good" or "bad" feelings of the body; the ones who bring food, warmth, safety, the "good" feelings. It is completely, utterly dependent on the actions of the "other" to take a "bad" feeling away, to bring a "good" feeling back to the body. This helplessness that needs the other—a mother, a father, a caretaker—to recover feelings of bodily pleasure carries inside it a frustration, an anger with its bodily pain. The hungry, wet, tired, cold, teething infant has only the language of cries and wails—angry protests against being left with the body suffering. The only thing to blame for the suffering of the body is, paradoxically, the one who brings comfort: The infant's anger at the bad feelings its body endures is directed against its most needed, cherished, loved object.

By age nine months, infants exhibit clear signs of this aggression—anger for being left alone, for the length of time it takes the loved ones to respond to their bodies' suffering. The infant is presented with an impossible contradiction: The most loved other, the one on whom it depends for all its good feelings, is also the only target for the infant's aggression, the only thing to blame for the bad feeling states of the body that is cold, hungry, wet, itching, burning, hurting.

The contradiction is too much for the infant. It has to split off the "good" and the "bad" in the loved one. To preserve as good the one who brings food, warmth, comfort, the infant has to find an object that can stand in as the bad thing into which it can pour all its anger, aggression, frustration, all the contradictory, unwanted feelings the infant has to endure. One of the most difficult things for a child to learn is that "good" and "bad" can exist in the same body, in the same object. That the mother is sometimes there to comfort and sometimes absent. That we sometimes feel pleasure and sometimes feel pain. That this is what it means to live in a body.

Our emotional growth requires learning how to integrate the "good" and the "bad" and tolerate ambivalence. This is a thing many people never learn. They have to split off all the bad elements, find an object to hold all the contradictions and confusions that overwhelm them. They need an "other"—the boy throws off what is "girl" in him, the Christian throws off what is "Jew" in her, the white throws off what is "black" in him. As Volkan puts it, "When kept inside, unintegrated, bad units threaten the self's cohesiveness; when put out there at a safe distance and used for comparison with good self- and object representations, they can enhance the sense of self" (1988, 33). A boy can feel strong, in control of the world, when he splits off what is "girl" in him, when he locates his inferior self at a safe distance, calls his projected split-off parts "girl," and feels, in comparison, superior. This is the same process at work in the making of all our "others."

This splitting-off of what is un-integrated in order to preserve a coherent feeling of a "good" self and the safe "us" is dangerous, though. Too often, that "other" that holds our split-off things, the bad feelings we cannot tolerate, becomes the "enemy." This process can be destructive when individuals create an "enemy" to hate, a scapegoat, something to blame for all the bad things that happen to them. We have all seen this—the relative, the colleague, the neighbor who always blames somebody else for his failures, who cannot see that his actions are part of what makes him suffer. Sometimes, this need to create the "enemy" other, the hated object to hold our split-off emotion, is deadly, as when Marc Lepine shot and killed fourteen women at the Ecole Polytechnique, an engineering school in Montreal. Shouting, "I want the women," he separated female from male students, yelled, "You're all a bunch of feminists!" and opened fire.

When dominant groups in a culture target cultural subgroups as their scapegoats, the splitting of "good" and "bad" can turn genocidal. En masse, people can turn to what their culture represents as "bad"— the black, the Jew, the Arab, the Muslim—and call them "evil." For an un-integrated split-off imaginary, then, things seem easy: The evil ones are the cause of all suffering. Kill them, wipe them out, and all the bad feelings will go away. We watched this in World War II–era Europe, epitomized in the Nazi concentration camp. We saw it in Rwanda, in Sierra Leone. We see it now in Darfur, the Congo, Sri Lanka. In the U.S. "war on terror." In all the countries presently at war, this discourse of the "evil other" makes people hungry to kill.

In all the years of our warring, we still have not learned this lesson: The "bad" feelings come from inside us, not from an evil other. Our violence brings more violence, our wars bring more war. We cannot achieve a "safe," "good" feeling state by finding a scapegoat, creating an enemy to kill. In a nuclear age, in the age of our imminent self-destruction, our survival depends on our psychic evolution, on our ability to integrate our "good" and our "bad" components. In Volkan's terms, we have to learn to understand how we create our "others" to hold our rage and learn to take back and integrate our projections.

We have to learn to see ourselves differently. Which means as "men" and "women." As members of "races" and religions and nations.

I am not saying this is easy. There are reasons that we hang on to our fear, rise up to defend ourselves from what we perceive to be attacking us. When that attack is immediate, present, in the form of the man with a gun, the torturer, the planes dropping bombs—what can it mean to change the way we think of ourselves and our enemies? It is not easy to say, in the face of invasion, "stand for peace." What would I do if I were a young woman in Baghdad, terrified by the militias—the U.S. Army, the Mehdi Army, the Badr Brigade? If I were a war orphan in Afghanistan, my playground a mine field? How, if my life clings to me, despite myself, while everybody I love has been killed—how am I to see in those who have destroyed my life and world something other than "enemy"? How am I to see myself as other than a victim of the savagery unleashed upon me?

But the man with the gun, the torturer, the planes dropping bombs—these things did not simply appear, mysteriously. They have evolved out of thousands of years of our invention. We invented everything. Our economies, our governments, our weapons. The roles we play as "men" and "women." We have lived thousands of years of bad ideas, and it is time that we change them.

I am not saying this is easy. I do not know, if I were one of those children in Angola, if I would have the strength, the courage, the integrity, to hold onto that little bit of peace in my heart. I know that, on the scale of things, I have had few hardships and great privileges—that the few hardships I have endured bore down upon me with a force so great that I needed the help of many, many people to lift the weight of shame-pain-rage and see possibilities for love, hope, peace. So, I do know—I really do know—that it is not easy to just change the way we see ourselves, the way we see others, the way we feel and think. I know this. But I also know that those children Nordstrom visited, the millions of people in the hundreds of organizations working for life, against the death drive, give me the responsibility of re-membering for the futures we need to create.

12

THE WORK OF LOVE

The only philosophy which can be responsibly practiced in the face of despair is the attempt to contemplate all things as they would present themselves from the standpoint of redemption. (Adorno 1978, 153)

If love is divine, it is not because it is alien or separated from us. Love, born from critical reinterpretation, is the affirmation of our relationship to the world and other people. (Oliver 2001, 221)

Encountering Love

In 1999, I went to the annual Women's Studies Conference at Southern Connecticut State University. The theme that year was Women's Rights and Human Rights. It was an amazing conference. Rigoberta Menchú, winner of the 1992 Nobel Peace Prize, gave the Keynote address. Speakers included women from the Revolutionary Association of the Women of Afghanistan and the Grandmothers of the Plaza de Mayo. These are women who have lived through war, horrific violence, the torture and murder of their loved ones. I was humbled by these women. At one point, Nora Strejilevich,[1] talking about being kidnapped and tortured

---

1 See Strejilevich 2002.

by Argentina's military junta, looked at the audience and asked: What compels a group of academics to come to her presentation, to listen to her story, to buy her book? What did her kidnap and torture have to do with us?

I felt my connection to her story through my father. Listening to her, I wondered if the men who tortured her were trained at the School of the Americas, the place where the United States trained such people as Augusto Pinochet and Manuel Noriega. I wondered what kind of training Frank had gotten as a military police officer, what the army had taught him about interrogation techniques. I wondered if the violence in our family was connected to violence he had witnessed—or committed—in Korea, in Vietnam. As a military police officer in the U.S. Army, what did "war" mean for him? And I wondered: What responsibility do I have for violences my father committed? What responsibilities do I have to people like Nora?

One night, when I was trying to explain my experience at this conference to my sister Zane, a fight broke out. Zane's first husband fought in Vietnam, where his leg was blown up by a land mine. In the 1980s, he died of liver cancer. In the mid-1990s, she married again; her second husband had served in the marines. Zane's entire life has been lived on military bases, and she is loyal to the men who defend her country. She was uncomfortable with my talking about the School of the Americas training South American militaries in the techniques for waging a "dirty" war, including torture. From her point of view, there is black and white, good and bad, and to get information about what the bad guys plan, the good guys have to be willing to get dirt on their hands. From Zane's point of view, I was attacking the people who were sacrificing themselves to defend me.

She was uncomfortable but trying hard to hear me. I was trying hard to explain what I was feeling. Her son, Kevin, came into the kitchen while we were talking. He muttered—under his breath, not directly to me, but loudly enough for me to hear it—"stupid bitch."

Angry, I confront him.

"What did you say?" Ready for a fight.

"Nothing, he didn't say anything." Zane trying to avoid a confrontation. Stop, don't talk, let's change the subject.

"Oh, no, I don't think so. I hardly think I'm letting that pass!" Me, wanting a knock-down drag-out fight, to hold Kevin responsible for

his words, to demand that his "stupid bitch" comment be acknowledged and condemned.

Kevin, three years younger than I was but six feet tall and 250
pounds, didn't say a word. Zane and her husband, Neil, had plans to go
out that night, and I had come to sit with Mother while they were gone.
While I was pushing Kevin for a confrontation, Zane and Neil fled the
house. It was too much to bear. Kevin wanted to leave too. But "stupid
bitch" and his desire to ignore it, to act like nothing had just happened,
snapped me.

E-mail to Angela, October 2006

He didn't say a word. I kept pushing him—"What did you
say? What did you say? 'Stupid bitch'?"

He just wanted to get out of the kitchen and away from
me, but I kept pounding him with my questions. I snapped.
Something in me just snapped. Like, the attempt to act as though
he had not just called me a stupid bitch, as though nothing had
happened, triggered me, and I could not, just simply could not,
stop; I wouldn't let Kevin go, wouldn't let him out of the kitchen.
He would have had to hit me to get past me, and it was probably
all he could do to not hit me.

At some level, maybe that's what I wanted, to have that kind
of beat-the-fucking-shit-out-of-each-other fighting that would
be the sign of the kind of pain and rage I was feeling. Finally he
said something, I forget what, but something along the lines of I
didn't know what I was talking about—about the School of the
Americas, where, of course, his friends have graduated from,
and where I think my brother's son did his sniper training. In
retrospect, I wonder: Was my nephew in sniper school the night
Kevin and I had this blowout?

So there's Kevin, saying, "You don't know what you're
talking about," and there I am, dripping contempt, responding,
"That's why you still don't have a real job and I have a Ph.D.?"
Those words, a knife stabbing him. And he managed, somehow,
to restrain himself—he didn't say a word in response, just moved
past me and out of the kitchen. I haven't seen him since.

My mother, who had been crying during most of this exchange, begging us to stop, was still crying when he left. But I was so righteous, so fucking righteous—I would have died in this fight rather than give it up. But I was also calm, really, really cold calm, the fucking cold calm that comes with adrenalin surging like crazy. I told Mother, from this really fucking cold calm overlying adrenalin surge, how this was the structure, exactly the structure, of Frank, and that I would not allow it, would not live it, anymore, ever. And do you know the only thing I remember her saying in this conversation? That I "gave as good as I got." It was the most bizarre thing, like even though she had been crying and saying, "Stop it. Please stop. Please just stop," she was registering enough of the conversation to keep track that I was at least "even," maybe even "winning"? And that some part of her maybe didn't want me to just "take it"?

So, I haven't seen Kevin since, and while I will periodically refer to this (which Zane never acknowledges) and joke about Kevin hating me (which Zane denies), I mostly leave it alone. There have been two or three similar moments: one when Neil and I got in a fight—a really really bad fight—about the KKK; he is from the South, generations of country Georgia, and for him the KKK means people in his church and extended family. For me, it is racist violence and hatred and killing. One day, Neil and I squared off over the KKK, me in go-off I'll-take-you-down mode. Zane and Kashif were there and, like Mother, upset by the force of our argument. It took a very long time to get over this fight.

But we did get over it. I realized, at some point, that Neil has never in his entire life actually talked to somebody who thinks the things I think. I shock him, challenge him, call his identity into question. And, even so, he tries—he really genuinely tries—to understand me. Realizing this, how he tries to think past where he stands and understand where I am coming from, humbled me. I felt how small my righteousness makes me. My heart opened to him, bringing with it a compassion that could temper the force of my judgment. It is easy to judge others—racist, sexist, xenophobic, closed-minded. But who was more narrow, more bigoted? Neil, feeling attacked by the force of my ideas and trying, still, to see me? Or me, wrapped up in my high-and-mighty, as though I were not guilty of precisely what I condemned?

I was humbled, and my heart broke open.

I am remembering all this today. And I am remembering Kevin. Thinking of him this morning, my heart started aching. My earliest memory of him is from Bahia Honda, in the Florida Keys, when he was five years old. Frank had just gotten out of the army, and he found a job at a state park, which is where we were living. Zane's first husband was in the hospital. He'd been in hospitals for a long time; first in Vietnam, where a land mine blew his leg up, and then in the States, for rehabilitation. Zane and Kevin came to live with us during the long months of skin grafts and physical therapy that he was undergoing. I think this was in 1973. By that time, Lily was living with us too. So there were nine of us—Mother, Frank, Mike, Leonard, Georgia, me, Zane, Kevin, Lily—living in a 720-square-foot, three-bedroom, single-wide trailer in a campground in the Florida Keys, waiting for Zane's husband to get out of the hospital with what was left of his leg.

Remembering Kevin at five years old is especially important today. My nerves are stretched so thin. The Lancet Report just came out—they estimate more than six hundred thousand Iraqis have died since we invaded their country. Three years into the war with Iraq (where I think, but Zane won't say for sure, that my nephew spent a year as a sniper) and the blind patriotism that allows all this killing is making me sick. Literally—I keep throwing up. Zane and Neil are out of town, and I have Mother for the weekend. Everybody around here is affiliated with Fort Stewart, invested in this "war." I want to scream and rage, to hold somebody accountable, to make them take back this horror we have unleashed in the world. But it is not Kevin; it is not Zane or Neil or Mother or any of the Fort Stewart soldiers who are to "blame." They want to believe that their government and their country are "good" and that they are "helping" the rest of the world. And how would they know any different? The news they watch, the papers they read, the places they work, the schools and churches they attend, the friends and family that influence them—they all say the same thing. They fill them up with stereotypes and sometimes outright lies. They make them afraid—afraid of people, cultures, religions that are foreign to them. The world they live in makes them believe that it is "us" or "them," that if "we" don't "get them," "over there," then "they" will come "here" and "get us." People in my own family really believe this.

People in my own family, who know and love Kashif. Who is from Pakistan. And Muslim. I am sick today from the ease with which normal people can be persuaded to fear, to hate, to kill. I feel desperate, as though it might be too late to stop the bloodbath we have caused. I am trying to calm down, to imagine the possibility of a world beyond this nightmare we are living.

I imagine Kevin, at five years old. What if Kevin had been able to grow up knowing Tahira, Kashif's mother? One of the kindest, gentlest souls I have ever met. A tiny Pakistani-American Muslim woman who was at Ronald Reagan Airport on September 11, 2001. Alone. She was flying in to visit me and Kashif, and Kashif was on his way to the airport to pick her up. I was still asleep. When Kashif heard the news on the radio about planes flying into the Twin Towers, he called to ask me to turn on the television. It still wasn't clear what had happened. Was this an accident? An attack? Then, the news about the Pentagon. Where was Tahira? Airspace was shut down, the airport evacuated, the entire country in a panic.

We spent the next twenty-four hours terrified, frantic. His sister and brother-in-law lived in New Jersey and worked in the city, his mother was in the no-man's land of evacuees from Ronald Reagan. All the phone circuits overloaded, and we couldn't get through to any of them.

When we found out that Kashif's mother and the rest of his family were all alive, and as safe as Muslim people in the States could be after 9/11, the frantic terror of those first few days gave way to the low-level, chronic fear I have lived with ever since. I am afraid of the rising tide of fear and hate that makes so many Americans see any Muslim, any brown-skinned person, as a potential "terrorist." I am afraid of the power we are giving our government—to listen to our phone calls, read our e-mails, arrest us without telling us why or letting anybody know where they are keeping us prisoner. I am afraid of the people who support our use of torture. I am afraid of a country that has lost so much of its own conscience that it does not rise up in protest against the very things it condemns in the rest of the world. I am afraid of the war we have become—threatening to invade North Korea, Iran, bullying the world and growing its hatred of us.

Today I am feeling desperate, and afraid, and throwing up.

I am afraid for people I love, and I love people who are part of the things that make me afraid.

So it is especially important that I remember Kevin today. I am remembering the last time I saw him and wishing I could have found a way of "standing up" that was not a beat-down/beat-back; I wish I could have found a way to refuse Kevin's "stupid bitch" that could have rescripted it. If I had been able to see that, underneath Kevin's lashing-out anger, there was a five-year-old waiting for his father to get out of the hospital and come home with what was left of his leg—if I had been able to see this, could I have found a way to act differently?

If I had been able to speak about Estela de Carlotto, president of the Grandmothers of the Plaza de Mayo, or Rosa Tarlovsky de Roisinblitt—if I could have explained how their daughters were kidnapped by government forces, how, since 1976, their lives have been a long, torturous lament for the daughters who were arrested, tortured, murdered—could he have heard that? Could I have spoken in a way that conveyed the pain of living all these years knowing that your daughter, who was pregnant when she was captured, delivered a baby who was stolen and raised by the same people who tortured and killed her? Could I have told their stories in a way that made him feel the pain of the dirty wars we helped wage?

Is it possible to find a path through anger—my own, righteous from one side, and Kevin's and Zane's and Neil's, righteous from another? Is it possible to see how anger can be the bravado-strutting that shields us from our fear and pain? Or the guilt we do not want to feel and so direct outward, onto the one who makes us feel guilty?

For so many years, I needed my anger to help me stand up against silence, denial, to take up the work of remembering against the work of forgetting. But anger cannot build connection, cannot lay the foundation for loving relation. For that, we need our compassion.

One the greatest gifts of my life—grace, I shall call it—has been these years living in daily relation to Mother, Zane, Neil. I have come to love them, to admire qualities in them that, in the years of my anger-holding-me-up, I failed to recognize. Mother, who has lived every day of her life in pain since that car wreck in the 1950s, shows me courage. One day Humera, Kashif's sister, said:

> *You know, you're really lucky, Lori. Most people who have been through what your mother has would be really depressed. She's in so much pain, she could be complaining all the time. She could be jealous of you because you have your health and she doesn't. She could be resentful that you can't imagine what it is like to live with the pain she has. If she were like that, she could really make your life miserable. But she's happy, and she wants to have a good time, and you're really lucky that she's like that.*

Until Humera said this, I didn't realize it. Humera, who has never even met my mother. Kashif's sister, a devout Muslim woman who admires my mother for her devout Catholicism. Who, from the outside looking in, could see what I could not.

Every day, my mother shows me courage. What it means to persevere. She shows me the pleasure of little things. She loves books, loves to watch golf and tennis, loves to go to lunch with her friends. She has a child's delight in the new clothes Zane buys her, in being well enough to go to the grocery store and search out new delectables at the deli counter. She loves ice cream—preferably chocolate. She loves. Despite everything, she loves life.

If Mother has the courage of persevering to teach me, Zane has the strength of oceans and mountains, the kind of loving that is like the horizon—it stretches out in every direction, as far as your eyes can see. As a child, she took care of Mike, Leonard, Georgia—her half-siblings from Mother's marriage to Frank. She was sixteen when Mother got pregnant with me and furious with her for having a seventh child—at forty-two, on-and-off crippled, Mother's pregnancy meant another child for Zane to raise. But it is the nature of her strength and her love to take on the work that needs to be done—like it or not.

Today I have to remember: Through all those years of my pain and my rage, despite all the ways that my presence attacks the things in which they believe, Mother, Neil, and Zane have found their ways to have compassion for me. I have to find a way to stand against this war that is not an "attack" on them. I have to find the way to show them my love, my respect, my gratitude—to show them this even as I say, as the way of being able to say, "I am opposed to this war. It has to stop."

13

CONCLUSION

Nineteen years after Frank left, I went to his childhood home in Lowell, Massachusetts, looking for something that could help me understand him. I wanted to find people who had known Frank so I could find out who he was to them. I wanted to learn something about the childhood he lived and the world he grew up in. I went looking for the stories that could help me understand the battles he fought with himself, the war he waged in his private world.

I started with an Internet search for the one person I could remember, Frank's brother, Thomas. I found Thomas's widow, Emma, and two of their daughters, Sarah and Lesa. Thomas had died the year before I went to Massachusetts. As with my trip to Oregon, I did not find my "father" in Massachusetts, but I did find something like perspective.

From Emma, Sarah, and Lesa, I have an image of Frank as generous, happy, the life of the party.

Emma: "Frank and Dee were always so much fun! We used to play cards, and I remember Dee drank Tom Collins. We always had such a good time when they came. I never laughed so much any other time."

Sarah: "Uncle Frank was my favorite. He was so funny. He always had funny stories, was always joking with us. Every time he came, he would take us to Kimball's for ice cream."

Sarah and Lesa: "We would always ask him to wiggle his ears! He could make his ears move back and forth, and it was so funny, we just couldn't stop laughing!"

Listening to the happy stories that Emma, Sarah, and Lesa were telling me, I tried hard to imagine the Frank whom they knew. This man—happy, fun-loving, generous, witty, charming—this man was my father too. Maybe a better part of him, maybe an ego ideal that he could not live up to in private. Maybe his downfall, the measure against which he hated the rest of himself. But a part of him, a dimension of his human-being-ness.

The stories of the good times they remembered, though, were shadowed by images of poverty, illegitimacy, domestic violence. It was Emma who told me about Frank's mother, my grandmother Velma—a woman whose name, if I had ever known it, I had forgotten. Emma told me this: Velma was married to a man named Ervin. Velma and Ervin had a large family, although Emma could not remember exactly how many children there were—maybe eleven, maybe thirteen? According to Emma, Ervin was violent, and Velma drank. Velma used to stay away from home for days at a time, binge drinking. She had lovers. One lover was a long-term affair, a man whom she thought was Frank and Thomas's real father.

"Did you know him?" I ask. "What was his name?"

"I forget his name. But I went to his funeral. We all did. Nobody talked about why, but we all went. Thomas and Frank look just like him, and I thought how this has to be him, the man Ida told me about."

"Ida?"

"Ida is Thomas and Frank's older sister. Thomas never told me about his father, but, one day, Ida did. For a time, Frank and Thomas lived with her—there were just too many children to take care of, and Ida felt bad for them. She said that Ervin wasn't their father, that their father was a man Velma was having an affair with. I believed her. At the funeral, I knew it had to be true. Thomas looked exactly like him."

Because Frank and Thomas looked so much alike, Emma believed that this same man must be father to both of them. She also thought that this might explain why they were so close—closer to each other than to any of the other children.

I wish I could have found Ida and asked her what she knew about my father, about this mystery of who his father was. But Ida was dead, as were most of the rest of Frank's brothers and sisters. The few who were still alive had left Massachusetts, and Emma never heard from them. Ida, long dead, took the name of the man whom she thought was Frank's father to the grave with her. Like so many other pieces of Frank's history, this no-name man, my maybe-grandfather, is a story that I cannot trace.

But Emma did have memories of my family and pieces of the story of Frank and Sally.

"I never really understood it," Emma said. "Nathan dying, and them carrying on like that. Thomas just couldn't take it."

Their entire lives, Frank and Thomas had been united by the bond of their no-name father. Thomas had always been loyal to Frank—through the investigation for molesting Margaret, through his return to the army, through all the years between Margaret and Sally. Until Nathan was dying, and Frank and Sally told him they were in love. Then, Thomas said, "You are sick. I don't want anything to do with you anymore."

After that, our families "lost touch." But Emma never forgot us. She brought out a box of old photographs, newspaper clippings, memories of "Frank and Dee" and their kids. She was present from the beginning, from the day Frank met my mother and they began courting. After "that business" with Margaret, when Frank went back in the army, he still visited Thomas and Emma—between duty stations, between wars, every time he had leave and could get back "home." In this intermittent way, Emma saw my brothers and sisters through their growing-up years, saw me when I was a child just back from Germany.

When I asked Emma what she remembered about "that business" with Margaret, she said, "I wasn't really sure what to make of it. Frank said she just wanted attention."

"What about Mother?" I asked.

"Dee? Well, I don't know. All I heard was that she wanted attention. I thought maybe it was hard, her father dying and all, and maybe she was confused."

"Do you remember an investigation?"

"Oh, yes. There was a big to-do. It was in the papers. The police were involved. But nothing came of it. Frank went back in the army, and that seemed to be the end of it. But then, when all that with Sally started, I wondered if there might not have been something to it after all. With Margaret, I mean."

July 11, 2001

At a Lowell Diner on Merrimack Street. Wanted coffee and breakfast, but also wanted a local diner, to get the feeling of the world my father knew. This is, of course, not really possible—all these years later, the most I can maybe get is a faint trace of the history that made Frank.

This is clearly a working-class establishment. My breakfast: eggs, pockets of butter pooling around the edges of the mostly cooked whites, fried potatoes, strong coffee. I don't mind so much that the edges of the floor here show the residue of years' worth of foot traffic, but I'm careful to keep my elbows off the tabletop and to keep my shirt—linen, off-white—from touching the wall beside me, both tabletop and wall being covered with a thin layer of the grease that saturates the air around the open kitchen's frytop. The breakfast is cheap: $3.99, with more potatoes than one person could possibly eat and unlimited refills on the coffee. Cheap enough for people whose bodies show the tangible signs of poverty to congregate at the counter over cups of coffee, to seek respite in the split-vinyl booths from whatever oppresses them in the outside world.

I would look out of place here in my $150 linen suit, except that it fits me so badly and I am so awkward in it that I am a good match for the local diner's crowd. The skirt is too long, so I've had to roll the elastic waistband over itself twice, just enough to hike the hemline above my ankles. The double-folded waistband bulges against the back of my shirt, forming a fat inner tube around my waist that has an odd symmetry with the dowager's hump on the old woman in the booth across from me.

This is where my father is from. The Lowell-Groton-Aire area north of Boston, where so many poor men my father's age spent years working in the Groton paper mill, breathing in asbestos and growing lung cancers. Where their widows try, sometimes successfully but mostly not, to stand up to the lawyers who deny any link between the asbestos in the mill and the cancers from which their husbands died. I try to imagine my father's father—Velma's lover, the man who has no name, my grandfather—in this diner, coming in off this street, taking his place next to the men returned from the First World War. But I can't really conjure the post–World War I scene because the army fatigues on the middle-age black man sitting at the counter keep reminding me of my father's wars: Korea and Vietnam.

All the other customers—a skinny old man, probably Irish, and a teenage couple hiding in the back corner booth—have bad teeth. The older customers have precious few teeth between them, and the young couple is in sore need of braces. All their bodies announce poverty and hardship in multiple other ways: skin and musculature marked by bad nutrition, slumped shoulders, and pained expressions. But I am especially struck by their teeth. Their teeth are like my sister Bernie's, who was born around here, spent her first ten years in this area, and then, after she got married, returned to Lowell with her husband, Randy. I don't remember a time when Bernie's teeth weren't rotted out of her mouth, jagged black half-stumps dotting the top and bottom of her front jaw, the black nubs at the back of her jaw ground down to the gum.

I never understood how Bernie could walk around with her teeth rotted out of her mouth. When I was young, I was ashamed of Bernie—ashamed of her tooth-rotted-out mouth, of her body showing the marks of our family's poverty. I wanted to hide from these things, to hide these things from the outside world—from teachers, children at school, the strangers who stared at the spectacle my family made when we went out. Mostly, I wanted to believe that I would never be Bernie—that I would somehow be able to keep my teeth, that I would be able to outrun the poverty and the hardship and all the things that lead to teeth rotting out of mouths. But in this diner, I see how easily black stumps take the place of white enamel. And I remember that, when I was fourteen, with pain shooting through my face, my friend Helen made my father let my mother take me to the dentist. I remember seeing a dentist only once before, when I was in the second grade and living on an army base in Fort Greely, Alaska. This shocked Helen. She could not imagine that some children did not go to the dentist every six months and had never heard of dental floss. As it turned out, I had two cavities. If Helen had not intervened, how long would it have taken those two unrestrained cavities to rot my mouth out?

More than anything, it is the half-empty mouths in this diner that move me, the normalcy of rotted-out teeth. It's all I can do not to cry in my eggs. My father's teeth were almost all rotted out of his mouth. My mother had dentures by her early fifties. So did my sister, Margaret. And Bernie, walking around with her black stumps. From this diner on Merrimack Street, I see how "normal" all this is.

———

Driving home from Lowell that summer, holding Emma and Sarah's stories, I tried to imagine the man Frank might have been. My memories and their stories all jumbled together, tangled up and tangling me: the bad teeth at the Merrimack Street diner, the cemetery where Velma was buried, Frank and Thomas as children, taking turns pushing each other in the river so they could drench their only school outfits and have an excuse to play hooky. Frank coming home after an inspection on the base and lining my sisters up for a "white glove test," the punishment he would mete out if he found dust anywhere in the house. The animal traps in the basement in Alaska, the gun Frank slept with.

For any one thing I might say about Frank, an opposite thing could be equally true. He was and was not the man whom I thought I remembered, was and was not either "good" or "bad." And I—I was and was not anything I thought myself to be, to have been. Driving down I-95 in the middle of the night, I felt my atoms spinning wildly, my electrons jumping orbit. Quantum physics: The objects we think of as "solid" are really made up of atomic particles, a whole microscopic universe of protons and electrons in a frenzy of motion. I remembered driving around campus at the University of Florida and wondering how all those atoms in the buildings around me could be spinning so fast and furiously yet give the illusion of solidity, as though they were perfectly still inside all those bricks covering all those buildings. Some days, I thought they might just spin out of control, and we'd see brick dissolve at any moment. That's how I felt driving home, full of Emma and Sarah and the fragments of my father I was trying to hold together. On that drive, I felt my atoms come untethered, leaving "me" a hundred different fragments scattered, scattering—an up-in-the-air self.

At some point, all those atoms dancing around were going to have to come down and reassemble into something; dispersed in air, I could only wait to see how my fragments would come together, form molecules, bond and reassemble. I observed my dispersed atoms with an interested detachment: Things could go a lot of different ways. Waiting to see what the pieces of "me" would assemble into, what shape my atoms would take, I cried my gratitude for my teachers: Helen, Ruth, Roberta, Bruce, Cristina, Masao, Andrew, Kathrin, Joyce, Elizabeth, Carolyn, Don, Kate, the friends and the family who have stood by me—I cried my gratitude for the many ways they had stood, seemingly so solid, sources of energy guiding my atoms back together, landing zones through which something called "Lori" could reassemble.

All those times in my life that I have been fragmented, floating, waiting to see how the pieces of me would come down and reassemble, things could have gone a lot of different ways. That "I" have taken *this* shape—a Ph.D., a college professor, a feminist, a social activist, a would-be Taoist—is so much a part of the teachers who have helped me. They gave me ideas about what kind of human being to be. And that gave me something for the pieces of me to reassemble around.

How many times did my father survive his electrons jumping orbit, his atoms dispersing and leaving him in fragments? Who did my father have to help his dispersing atoms bond? What was there to help him reassemble into a "man"? What stable objects, people, things could have provided the structure around which the million pieces of himself up in the air could come back together? How could the million pieces of my father have come down differently?

During the entire drive, I felt that, under different circumstances, Frank's atoms could have assembled into me, and mine could have assembled into him. I spent twenty-four years running, racing, frenziedly working my way out of enlisted-army quarters, trailer parks, working full-time at school and at my jobs. I lived on three and four hours of sleep during the week, driven by an urgency, a life-or-death need to finish a class project, finish a semester, pay off debt, "accomplish" this or that or the other. And isn't this how Frank lived? Urgent, life or death? Spinning wildly, trying to keep up with his own atoms?

Was the shame of his poverty, his illegitimacy, his desire to "be somebody" behind Frank's desire to be a soldier, his violence, his fantasies of killing? And aren't we the same in this? Isn't it the shame I was running from that drove me through school, to an education and a "professional" job, something I could be "proud" of?

I have made my life in opposition to Frank's but, by virtue of that fact, remain linked to his trajectory. Our lives: tangles of atoms spinning wildly, looking deceptively like something "solid."

In the little life of "normal" that I have made, I try to learn, by looking at my legacy from Frank, how to take responsibility for what he left me. I can never inhabit my body as if Frank did not write himself into me. Inscribed as I have been by Frank's unthought desire, I bear witness to the potentially violent, consuming side of our nature. As witness, I have the responsibility of what Kelly Oliver calls "critical reinterpretation"—the way of re-membering that forges love through our compassionate connections to other people and to the world. This way of loving is not blind: It turns into the worst of who we are and returns a vision of the best that we can be.

Carolyn Nordstrom, who has spent twenty years on the front lines of war, turns into the worst of what is human—the most horrifying violences of the bloodiest wars—and returns to us a vision of love at work: the children in Angola, the best of us. The future we have to remember demands that we see both.

One of Nordstrom's sources in Mozambique helps us in this task:

You want to know why people join this war? Look around you. A guy is walking down the dusty road and a nice big car flashes by him, leaving him eating dust, and he thinks, "Why him and not me?" And he knows the answer is that the guy in the car is on the right side of politics—the side that controls the goods. He knows he is on the wrong side. No matter how smart he is, no matter what a good worker he is, no matter what his ambitions, he won't get where he wants to go. The other guy, the guy with connections to the politicos in power, not him, will get the job. . . . And that reality stretches out in front of him to cover his whole life: there's no changing the politics of it. It won't be him riding in that car; he'll be walking the rest of his life. So he eats that other guy's dust and he thinks, "Why not join the opposition and fight, that's the only way I can improve my lot in life." (2004, 77)

It is so banal, so everyday—turning to the identity of "soldier" for the possibility of dignity, value, meaning. Isn't this what my father did? Use his soldier's uniform to prove his worth, his importance? Did he feel himself, all dressed up in his army green, to be smart, beautiful, useful? And is that not what I am doing too? Using my scholar's robes to prove my worth, my value? All dressed up in university, performing smart, beautiful, useful? Frank and I in our different uniforms: army green and university.

But that soldier's uniform was not, after all, the smart-beautiful-useful that could save him. And it cannot save the rest of us, either. It is not our militaries that make us "safe" or "protect" us. Our wars breed each other, over and over and over. Proliferating, escalating, until, finally, we are on the brink of causing our own extinction. Ninety percent of the people killed in modern wars are civilians (UN Security Council 2009). Every war on the planet has international players fueling it—the gun runners; the gem smugglers; the international armies that train various factions; the human traffickers; the corporations, such as Lockheed Martin and Halliburton, that make fortunes off people's suffering. Starvation, refugees, war orphans. Malaria, dysentery, contagious diseases. Buildings bombed, cities in ruin, no electricity, no water, no schools, no medicine.

We have become so accustomed to this state of affairs that, as Tzvetan Todorov writes, "We have resigned ourselves to wars, both present and future. We have grown used to seeing extreme poverty all around us and not thinking about it" (1997, 253). Our indifference stems in part from our inability to perceive any possibility for action—we do not think we can do anything about the suffering that, too overwhelming to acknowledge, we pretend does not exist. The forces structuring our lives—global economics that are too complicated to follow, political histories of which we are ignorant—are too big to grasp or to see a way out of. We focus on the only thing that we can really see: our individual survival and relative well-being. When we do this, though, we are consolidating the power of the very forces that trap us in violence (130). In this way, we become, as Todorov shows us, unwitting accomplices of the systems of killing (131).

Following Todorov's analysis, totalitarianism shows us that "at the end of the path of indifference and conformity lies the concentration camp" (1997, 253)—or Abu Ghraib. Dachau, Abu Ghraib—these do not come into being through the actions of just a few "evil" men. For such things to exist, it is "necessary that the vast majority stand aside, indifferent; of such behavior, as we know well, we are all of us capable" (139). We step aside and leave the road clear for atrocities because we do not want to see what disturbs our own comfort. If, despite ourselves, we catch a glimpse of things we do not want to see, we tell ourselves nothing we can do will make any difference (139). But we are, by nature, "neither good nor evil, or else [we] are both at once; selfishness and altruism are equally innate" (139).

Recognizing that "it is as easy to do good as to do evil," Todorov proposes a code of "ordinary moral values and virtues, one commensurate with our times" (1997, 291). To counter hate, war, violence, "we need not imitate saints. Nor need we fear monsters; both the dangers and the means with which to neutralize them are all around us" (291). We have invented the forms, structures, and tools that make the violence around us. We are just as capable of inventing the forms, structures, and tools of peace. We have spent so many centuries cultivating our capacity for war that we can no longer see the possibility of a world without it. But we have as much capacity for connection, compassion, and loving relation as we do for killing, hatred, and violence. We have had to work hard to make war—train, practice, prepare, sacrifice. We have to do the same thing to make peace—train our hearts and our minds, practice in our day-to-day lives.

War depends on fear of oppression, a belief in force, and a willingness to use violence. Soldiers fight wars and civilians support them because they fear losing what they have and hope to gain something they don't. War also depends on placing these fears and beliefs in a framework that specifies friend and foe, political alliance and alienation. When citizens hold these fears and support these beliefs, and when they are willing to use force in their name, war remains paramount. So peace begins when people find violence the worst threat of all. (Nordstrom 2004, 181)

I find violence the worst threat of all. I am praying that we can re-member a future—re-member as a creative act, as a way of imagining what, as human beings, we *can be.*

References

Adorno, Theodor. 1978. *Mimima moralia: Reflections from damaged life*. London: Schocken Books.

Associated Press. 2006. Hearing to begin for five U.S. soldiers in Mahmoudiya rape-slaying. *USA Today,* August 5, 2006. Available at www.usatoday.com/news/world/2006-08-05-iraq-rape-trial_x.htm (accessed October 16, 2008).

Brennan, Teresa. 2004. *The transmission of affect*. Ithaca, NY: Cornell University Press.

Buhaug, Halvard, Scott Gates, Håvard Hegre, and Håvard Strand. 2007. Global trends in armed conflict. Centre for the Study of Civil War, International Peace Research Institute, Oslo (PRIO). Available at www.regjeringen.no/nn/dep/ud/kampanjer/refleks/innspill/engasjement/prio.html?id=492941 (accessed October 16, 2008).

Bureau of Justice Statistics. 2005. Family violence statistics: Including statistics on strangers and acquaintances. Available at http://bjs.ojp.usdoj.gov/content/pub/pdf/fvs.pdf (accessed December 20, 2009).

Carey, Benedict. 2006. Study links military duty in Iraq to lapse in mental ability. *New York Times,* August 2, 2006. Available at www.nytimes.com/2006/08/02/health/psychology/02psych.html?ex=1184817600&en=d155952752bf2658&ei=5070 (accessed October 16, 2008).

Carter, Rita. 1999. *Mapping the mind*. Berkeley: University of California Press.

Caruth, Cathy. 1996. *Unclaimed experience: Trauma, narrative, and history*. Baltimore: Johns Hopkins University Press.

Centers for Disease Control and Prevention, Department of Health and Human Services. Violence prevention. Available at www.cdc.gov/ncipc/dvp/dvp.htm (accessed December 20, 2009).

Connell, R. W. 2007. Masculinities, the reduction of violence and the pursuit of peace. In *Gender violence: Interdisciplinary perspectives.* Eds. Laura O'Toole, Jessica R. Schiffman, and Margie L. Kiter Edwards, 33–40. New York: New York University Press.

Da Costa, Rosa. 2006. The administration of justice in refugee camps: A study of practice. Legal and Protection Policy Research Series. Office of the United Nations High Commissioner on Refugees. Available at www.unhcr.org/pro-tect/PROTECTION/44183b7e2.pdf (accessed October 2008).

Damasio, Antonio. 1999. *The feeling of what happens: Body and emotion in the making of consciousness.* Orlando: Harvest Books.

———. 2003. *Looking for Spinoza: Joy, sorrow, and the feeling brain.* Orlando: Harvest Books.

Das, Veena. 2007. *Life and words: Violence and the descent into the ordinary.* Berkeley: University of California Press.

Dorner, Jimmy R., and James L. Graff. Canada the man who hated women. *Time,* December 18, 1989. Available at www.time.com/time/magazine/arti-cle/0,9171,959361,00.html (accessed December 20, 2009).

Enloe, Cynthia. 2002. Demilitarization—Or more of the same? In *The post-war moment: Militaries, masculinities, and international peacekeeping.* Ed. Cynthia Cockburn, 22–32. London: Lawrence and Wishart.

Felman, Shoshana. 1992. Education and crisis, or the vicissitudes of teaching. In *Testimony: Crises of witnessing in literature, psychoanalysis, and history.* Eds. Shoshana Felman and Dori Laub, 1–56. New York: Routledge.

Global Fund for Women (GFW). Trafficking. Available at www.globalfundforwo-men.org/cms/hot-topics/trafficking/trafficking.html (accessed October 16, 2008).

Grandmothers of the Plaza de Mayo. Available at www.derechos.org/human-rights/grandmothers.html (accessed December 20, 2009).

Grossman, Dave. 1995. *The psychological cost of learning to kill in war and society.* New York: Little, Brown.

Hayner, Priscilla. 2002. *Unspeakable truths: Facing the challenges of truth commis-sions.* New York: Routledge University Press.

Hellman, Christopher, and Travis Sharp. 2008. The FY 2009 Pentagon (DOD) defense budget spending request. Available at www.armscontrolcenter.org/policy/securityspending/articles/fy09_dod_request/ (accessed October 26, 2009).

Jelin, Elizabeth. 2003. *State repression and the labors of memory.* Trans. Judy Rein and Marcial Godoy-Anativia. Minneapolis: University of Minnesota Press.

Kandel, Eric. 2007. *In search of memory: The emergence of a new science of mind.* New York: W. W. Norton.

Kaufman, Michael. 2007. The construction of masculinity and the triad of men's violence. In *Gender violence: Interdisciplinary perspectives.* Eds. Laura O'Toole, Jessica R. Schiffman, and Margie L. Kiter Edwards, 33–55. New York: New York University Press.

Kristof, Nicholas D. 2008. The weapon of rape. *New York Times*, June 15, 2008. Available at www.nytimes.com/2008/06/15/opinion/15kristof.html (accessed December 12, 2009).

Laub, Dori. 1992. Bearing witness, or the vicissitudes of listening. In *Testimony: Crises of witnessing in literature, psychoanalysis, and history*. Eds. Shoshana Felman and Dori Laub, 57–74. London: Routledge, 1992.

Levi, Primo. 1988. *The drowned and the saved*. New York: Summit Books.

MacKinnon, Katherine. 2006. Interview with Stuart Jeffries. *Guardian*, April 12, 2006. Available at www.guardian.co.uk/world/2006/apr/12/gender.politics-philosophyandsociety (accessed October 16, 2008).

National Coalition against Domestic Violence. 2007. Domestic violence facts. Available at www.ncadv.org/files/DomesticViolenceFactSheet(National).pdf (accessed December 12, 2009).

Nordstrom, Carolyn. 1996. Visible wars and invisible girls, shadow industries, and the politics of not-knowing. *International Feminist Journal of Politics* 1 (1): 14–33.

———. 2004. *Shadows of war: Violence, power, and international profiteering in the twenty-first century*. Berkeley: University of California Press.

Oliver, Kelly. 2001. *Witnessing beyond recognition*. Minneapolis: University of Minnesota Press.

Shah, Anup. World military spending. 2009. Global Issues Online. Available at www.globalissues.org/article/75/world-military-spending (accessed December 11, 2009).

Strejilevich, Nora. 2002. *A single, numberless death*. Trans. Cristina de la Torre. Charlottesville: University Press of Virginia.

Todorov, Tzvetan. 1997. *Facing the extreme: Moral life in the concentration camps*. New York: Holt Paperbacks.

UN High Commissioner for Refugees. 2008. 2007 global trends: Refugees, asylum-seekers, returnees, internally displaced and stateless persons. Available at www.unhcr.org/statistics/STATISTICS/4852366f2.pdf (accessed October 16, 2008).

UNICEF. 2007. Child protection from violence, exploitation and abuse: Children in conflict and emergencies. Available at www.unicef.org/protection/index_armedconflict.html (accessed May 13, 2009).

UN Security Council. 2009. Security Council, expressing deep regret over toll on civilians in armed conflict, reaffirms readiness to respond to their deliberate targeting: Adopted unanimously, Resolution 1894 (2009) demands strict compliance with international humanitarian, human rights, refugee law. Department of Public Information, News and Media Division. Available at www.un.org/News/Press/docs/2009/sc9786.doc.htm (accessed December 11, 2009).

U.S. Department of State. 2007. Trafficking in persons report. Office of the Under Secretary for Democracy and Global Affairs and Bureau of Public Affairs. Available at www.state.gov/documents/organization/82902.pdf (accessed October 16, 2008).

Vasterling, Jennifer J., Ph.D.; Susan P. Proctor, D.Sc.; Mike Amoroso, M.D., MPH; Robert Kane, Ph.D.; Timothy Heeren, Ph.D.; and Roberta F. White, Ph.D. 2006. Neuropsychological outcomes of army personnel following deployment to the Iraq war. *Journal of the American Medical Association* 296:519–529.

Volkan, Vamik. 1988. *The need to have enemies and allies: From clinical practice to international relationships.* Northvale, NJ: Jason Aronson.

Wiesel, Eli. 1982. *Dawn.* New York: Bantam Books.

Wikipedia. Abeer Qassim Hamza al-Janabi. Available at http://en.wikipedia.org/wiki/Abeer_Qassim_Hamza (accessed December 20, 2009).

Women's International League for Peace and Freedom. 2007. Peacekeeping watch: Monitoring sexual exploitation and abuse by UN peacekeepers and the efforts of the international community to respond. Available at www.peacewomen.org/un/pkwatch/pkwatch.html (accessed October 2008).

Zarkov, Dubravka, and Cynthia Cockburn, eds. 2002. *The post-war moment: Militaries, masculinities, and international peacekeeping.* London: Lawrence and Wishart.

Web Sites

Antiwar.com. Available at www.antiwar.com.

Coalition for Peace Action. Available at www.peacecoalition.org.

Code Pink. Available at www.codepink4peace.org.

Fellowship of Reconciliation. Available at www.forusa.org.

Free the Slaves. Available at www.freetheslaves.net.

Gender DynamiX. Available at www.genderdynamix.co.za.

Global Action to Prevent War. Available at www.globalactionpw.org.

Global Fund for Women. Available at www.globalfundforwomen.org/cms.

Global Peace Initiative. Available at www.globalpeacenow.com.

Grandmothers for Peace International. Available at www.grandmothersforpeace
   .org.

Grandmothers of the Plaza de Mayo. Available at www.derechos.org/human-
   rights/grandmothers.html.

His Holiness, the 14th Dalai Lama. Available at www.dalailama.com.

Human Rights Watch. Available at www.hrw.org.

International Foundation for Gender Education. Available at www.ifge.org.

International Peace Bureau. Available at http://ipb.org.

Iraq Veterans against the War. Available at http://ivaw.org.

Men Stopping Violence. Available at www.menstoppingviolence.org/index.php.

Mouths Wide Open: The Army Men Project. Available at www.mouthswideopen
   .org/armyinfo.shtml.

National Peace Foundation. Available at www.nationalpeace.org.

Parents, Families, and Friends of Lesbians and Gays. Available at http://commu-
   nity.pflag.org/Page.aspx?pid=194&srcid=-2.

Pathways to Peace. Available at http://pathwaystopeace.org.

Peace Boat. Available at www.peaceboat.org/english/index.html.

Peace Factory Cyberworks. Available at www.peacefactory.com/leaders.

Plum Village. Available at www.plumvillage.org.

Quakers: Religious Witnesses for Peace since 1660. Available at www.quaker.org.

Search for Common Ground. Available at www.sfcg.org.

TrueMajority. Available at www.truemajority.org.

United for Peace and Justice. Available at www.unitedforpeace.org.

Veterans for Peace. Available at www.veteransforpeace.org.

Women in Black. Available at www.womeninblack.org.

Women's International League for Peace and Freedom. Available at www.wilpf
.org and www.wilpf.int.ch.

Women to Women International. Available at www.womentowomeninternatio-
nal.org.

Index

Lily, 56, 91, 173; and the car wreck pattern, 98; checks sent to Frank by, 38–39; Frank reported to police by, 30, 54, 58, 75; and Frank's childhood trauma, 94; Margaret viewed by, 90; and relationship with Frank, 87–88, 94

Lisa, 113, 118

Lori, *33, 57;* and anger at Mother, 35–36; and the canceled checks, 38–39; clothes purchased for, by Frank, 32; comparing self to Georgia, 20, 21; divorce of, 99; education of, 11, 28, 97, 98; facts about, on birth certificate, 29–30; and fear since 9/11, 175; and fighting the effects of Frank, 73–74; and first memory of Frank, 30, 38; and forgetting, 41–42, 43, 45; and Frank and Sally's relationship, 11–18, 20–22, 24, 25; as Frank's accomplice, 19, 20, 24, 34, 36, 106, 112; and Frank's self-pity, 111–112; ghosts of, 33–34, 35, 51, 76, 80; as the good girl, 18, 96, 99; guilt felt by, 32, 36, 37, 95, 96, 99, 100, 106; haunted house of, 39–40, 51, 97, 112; and integration of fragmented selves, 185–186, 187; Jenny abandoned by, 95, 96, 99; life with Frank re-created by, 5, 6, 26–27, 28, 35, 53; and memories of Frank, 13–14, 30, 31–32, 38, 73, 103; Mother abandoned by, 26, 34; and nightmares, 52–53, 71–72, 74–75, 78–80, 99; and panic and anxiety attacks, 5, 6; and the path through anger, 176; and return to Florida, 5, 35–41; and search for Frank in Oregon, 98, 100–103; and search for Frank's childhood, 179; shame felt by, 116, 186; silence of, 24, 60, 112–114; and skin shudders, 52, 53; standing up to Frank, 97–98, 106–107, 109; students of, whose lives are shaped by violence, 162–163; teaching high school, 112, 114–116, 122; and unconscious processing of sensory information, 48–49; as witness, 186. *See also* Amy family

love: and the children in Angola, 163–164, 168; and critical reinterpretation, 169, 186; and mourning, 160; and re-membering a future, 162; work of, 163–165

Lowell, Massachusetts, 179, 182–183, 184

MacKinnon, Katherine, 153

Margaret, 23–24, 38; bad teeth of, 184; and car accident, 56, 89, 91, 98; children of, 88, 90–91, 100; and the family script, 94, 95, 98; Frank viewed by, 58–59; and Jenny's death, 98, 100; and Lily, 87, 88, 90; marriages of, 90; and memories of Frank, 54–55, 56, 57, 58–59; molested by Frank, 23, 30, 54, 57, 58, 89, 91, 181–182; and Mother's depression, 57, 59; Mother's life saved by, 56, 89, 91; as remembered by Emma, 181; silence of, 59, 60, 89; and Simon, 91, 100. *See also* Amy family

Marge, 120

Maria, 141–144, 145

Mark, 15, 19

Marnie, 88, 94, 95, 103; sent to St. Louis, 90, 91

Marvin, 97

masculinity: battle and sex as milestones in, 137, 146; defined as the negation of the feminine, 127, 128, 137, 148, 165; as the foundational fantasy of social and cultural structures, 127–128; fragility of, and violence against women, 152; as ideology, 152; in the military, 128, 137, 146; rescripting of, 152–153

meaning: and cognitive and linguistic development, 77–78; and dreams, 75–76, 77, 79; and memory, 59; mourning the death of, 80; multiple, 81–82; as process, 76; and witnessing, 84

Melissa, 15, 19, 109

memory: and the amygdala, 47; exemplary, 8–9, 160–161; literal, 8, 160; and meaning, 59; and neural stimuli, 47–48; stabilizing, 48; storage of, in neurons, 6, 46; and truth, 4, 5, 53, 60

memory project, 9

memory wars, 5, 53

Menchú, Rigoberta, 169
Mike, 24, 30, *57*, 173; and Jenny and Lori's desire for confrontation, 101; Mother assisted by, 26, 36, 109, 110; raised by Zane, 177; and relationship with Frank, 31, 124. *See also* Amy family
militarization: alternatives to, 151–152; and the fetishization of femininity, 148–149; of society, 147–148
military; age of recruitment for, 105, 106; everyday violence in, 129–130; and identity, 2, 131–133, 137; initiation rituals in the, 128–129; masculinity in, 128, 137, 150; and safety, 188; U.S. expenditures for, 155. *See also* U.S. Navy
Modell, Arnold, 61
Mother, *57*; abandoned by Lori, 26, 34; bad teeth of, 184; canceled checks kept by, 38–39; car accidents and, 34, 56, 89, 98, 109, 110, 176; children of, 29–30; compared to Lori, 159; compassion of, for Lori, 177; depression of, 57, 59; and the family script, 95, 98; and Frank and Sally, 14, 16, 20–21, 22, 23; and life with Frank, 57–58; and life with Patrick, 55–56, 57; Lori's compassion and admiration for, 176–177; in Lori's dreams, 80–81; and Lori's fight with Kevin, 171, 172; and Margaret's silence, 54, 58; and memories of Frank, 37–38, 43, 58, 59; poverty of, 26, 36, 37, 38, 106; as remembered by Emma, 179, 181; silence of, 60, 89; and the war in Iraq, 173–174, 177. *See also* Amy family
mourning: connections re-established through, 9; and the death of meanings, 80; and options, 161–162; pain acknowledged by, 9, 160; and re-membering a future, 9, 161; and witnessing, 159, 160
Mozambique, 138, 139, 186–187
murder statistics, 153

narrative theory, 3
Nathan, 11, 12, 181
nationalism, 8, 150; alternatives to, 151–152
nation making, 150, 151
Need to Have Enemies and Allies, The (Volkan), 165–166
Neil, 171, 176, 177; fight with Lori, 172–173; and the war in Iraq, 173–174, 177
neural stimuli and memory, 47–48
neuroscience, 46
9/11, 153, 174–175
Nordstrom, Carolyn, 138, 163, 168, 186
Noriega, Manuel, 170

object relations theory, 165–166
O'Brien, Patrick, 55–56, 57, 91
Office of the UN High Commissioner for Refugees (UNHCR), 156
oiling, 8, 130
Oliver, Kelly, 186
other, 166–167

patriarchy, alternatives to, 151–152
Patrick (O'Brien), 55–56, 57, 91
peace: invention of forms, structures, and tools to create, 188; peace movements, 151; and the practice of self-reflection, analysis, and compromise, 10; and re-membering a future, 189; training and practice in, 188; and the transformation of the gender order, 165, 167; and violence as the worst threat of all, 189
Pinochet, Augusto, 170
poisonous knowledge, 159–160, 161
pollywogs, 128–129
pornography: and Abu Ghraib, 124, 126, 127; in Fort Greely basement, 121–122; and the link between sex and killing, 147; and Mozambique story, 138–139; and our forgetting, 139
posttraumatic stress disorder, 77
Prechtel, Martin, 141
prostitution, 156

race, 153
Randy, 183
rape, 126, 147, 151, 162; and exemplary memory, 160–161; and nation making, 151; and oiling, 130; statistics for, 153; as

Lori E. Amy is Associate Professor in the Department of Writing and Linguistics at Georgia Southern University.